"God is One, He is the Creator,
He is forever Victorious."

"I love a Sikh's disciplined way of life,
not the Sikh."

Sikh Code of Conduct
(Summarised Version)

Translated by,

Harjinder Singh,
Sukha Singh & Jaskeerth Singh

Published by Akaal Publishers

www.akaalpublishers.com

6th Edition December 2020

ISBN 978-1-9996052-4-7

Dedicated to

Baba Takhur Singh Jee Khalsa (1915 – 2004)

Who was a shining example of a Khalsa

Foreword to Fifth Edition
Further explanations have been made to aid the readers understanding of the concepts and practices explained herein. This has been done throughout the publication as a result of readers feedback.

Harjinder Singh, March 2016

Foreword to Fourth Edition

With the grace of Sri Guru Granth Sahib Jee the fourth edition of the summarised version of the Gurmat[1] Rehat Maryada/Code of Conduct has been completed. This edition is aimed at a global audience, for Sikhs and non-Sikhs to get an insight into what the Sikh Way of Life entails. The Code of Conduct may seem harsh and very hard to put into practice but it is an ideal way of living that very few gifted souls realise. If one were to put all the teachings into practice then self-realisation is attained and abode with God is guaranteed.

This fourth edition has the added benefit of 'Gurbani da Adab' – 'Respecting Gurbani' - being added to this publication. This has been translated by Bhai Sukha Singh and Bhai Jaskeerth Singh, it can be found at the end of this publication. This is a much needed addition which can help the readers learn about Respecting Gurbani in the appropriate way. Previously only a summary of 'Respecting Gurbani' was included in previous editions, now both the summary and full version can be read at the end of this publication.

This fourth edition is by no means perfect and I urge the readers to give us their comments and questions by emailing us at info@akaalpublishers.com. I have tried my best to make the

---

[1] Gurmat – is the knowledge of the Guru, Guru means enlightener or teacher. Herein Gurmat will always refer to the knowledge taught by the Sikh Gurus.

document as simple as possible and minimise jargon, so all levels of reader may easily understand the path of the Guru. I urge the Sangat to forgive our shortcomings in translation. The translators and sevadars who helped in completing this task, hope the readers will benefit from the additional information that has been added.

I would like to thank Baba Takhur Singh Jee for blessing me with leading on the translation of this tract and would like to give a brief mention and thanks to all the Singhs that helped in completing this work. First and foremost I would like to thank Giani SurJeet Singh Jee 'Sodhi/Bairagi' who has been a source of knowledge throughout the compilation of all editions. Other Singhs who helped with translations and editing were Giani Davinder Singh Jee (Batala), Giani Jatinder Singh Jee, Giani Jangbir Singh Jee, Giani Baldev Singh Jee Sodhi, Giani Kuldeep Singh Jee Bhagat, Bhai Baldeep Singh Jee, Bhai Sukhraj Singh and Bhai Harpartap Singh Jee.

The existing foreword & gratitude expressed for assistance in compiling the Respecting Gurbani section has been added at the start of that section – please read that to see the acknowledgements.

Finally, I would like to take personal responsibility for any errors in any of the publication, including the 'Respecting Gurbani' section – as I made the final edits. I beg for forgiveness for any of my editorial shortcomings and express thanks to Bhai Sukha Singh & Bhai Jaskeerth Singh for giving permission for use of 'Respecting Gurbani' in this 4th edition of the Code of Conduct.

Your servant,

Harjinder Singh
Walsall, England
April 2015

Translators Introduction

The Rehat Maryada (Sikh Code of Conduct) has been translated with the great grace of Sri Guru Granth Sahib Jee. The translators and sevadars who have worked on this publication are forever grateful to the Gurus and the disciplined Gursikhs who have lived and acted accordingly to the Rehat Maryada,[2] explained herein.

The Sevadars of this publication feel that it is pertinent to mention that we ourselves are endeavouring to live up to the high standards of the Rehat Maryada. The discipline of a Khalsa is indeed *"Sharper than the Khanda (double-edged sword) and finer than a hair"* (Sri Guru Amar Das, Anand Sahib), this Rehat Maryada is a moral standard that all Sikhs should aim to achieve. We pray that Satguru blesses us and all those that read this Rehat Maryada to live up to the high morality and spirituality explained within it.

We are forever grateful to Baba Thakur Singh Jee, Jathedar of Damdami Taksaal, who gave us permission to translate this tract. We are grateful to all the 'gupt'[3] Singhs/Singhnia who have laboured at proof-reading the numerous editions and have given invaluable suggestions.

We translated the Maryada as we felt there was a void in all present English publications, as there was no one tract/book that covered Rehat effectively. The books that are related to Rehat, have very few references to Gurbani or historical Rehatmaryadas/Rehat Namas[4] of the times of the Gurus.

---

[2] Code of Conduct
[3] Anonymous
[4] Code of Conducts

The Importance of Gurmukhi/Panjabi

We feel that all Sikhs must attempt to learn Gurmukhi, the script and language of Gurbani that was created by our beloved Gurus. This translation does not even come near the original in Panjabi, as effective translations into English of Gurbani/Panjabi cannot be achieved. We can get near but cannot get the full meaning or essence from a translation. To get the full essence of Gurbani and Sikhi we must endeavour to learn Panjabi and Gurmukhi, and this will open many pathways to knowledge for us.

The aim of the translation is to inform and inspire the readers. We pray that Guru Sahib may bless all the readers with the skills of the Gurmukhi language.

We beg for forgiveness from Sahib Sri Guru Granth Sahib Jee for any mistakes that have been made in translation, publication and preparation of the Rehat Maryada. We pray that Guru Sahib and the Sadh Sangat (Holy Congregation) can forgive our shortcomings and give us the fortitude and strength to continue serving the Khalsa Panth.

Harjinder Singh

Gurfateh Jee

CONTENTS

	PAGE
The Five Ceremonies	1
1. Birth Ceremony	1 - 3
2. Education Ceremony	4 - 6
3. Amrit Ceremony	7 - 9
3.1 The provision of Amrit & the selection of the Panj Pyare	9 - 11
3.2 Ardas for the worthiness of the Amrit Ceremony Sevadars	11 - 12
3.3 Questioning of initiates	12 - 14
3.4 Ardas to prepare Amrit	15
3.5 Preparing Amrit	15 - 17
3.6 Ardas for the completion of the preparation of the Amrit	17
3.7 Bestowing Amrit	17 - 19
3.8 Mool Mantar and the manifestation of Gurmantar in the initiates	19 - 21
3.9 Teachings given by the Panj Pyare	21 - 24
3.10 Five Kakkaars	25 - 31
3.11 The Four Cardinal Sins	32 - 40
3.12 The Five Takhats (Thrones) of the Khalsa	40 - 41
3.13 Four Foundations	41 - 42

	3.14	The Four Colours of the Khalsa	42
	3.15	Five groups of people who are not to be associated with	44 - 46
	3.16	Five not to be associated with	47 - 48
4.		Wedding Ceremony/Anand Karaj	49 - 57
	4.1	Paath, Parkarma and practical teachings	57 - 69
5.		Death Ceremony	70 - 74
6.		Respecting Gurbani (summarised)	75 - 81
	6.1	Summary of the Rehat of Sri Guru Granth Sahib Jee, Akhand Paath & Sehaj Paath	81 - 84
	6.2	Raagmala	84 – 86
7.		Respecting Gurbani (Full Version)	87 - 126
		Annexes	127
	•	Preparing Karah Parshad/Degh	128 – 130
	•	Glossary	131 - 142

The Five Ceremonies

There are five ceremonies of life that most Sikhs undergo. These ceremonies explain what a Sikh should do at these pertinent points in life. The following is a brief description of each ceremony and what should occur from cradle to grave for a Sikh.

1) BIRTH CEREMONY / JANAM SANSKAR (first ceremony)

When God blesses a couple with a child, at this auspicious moment the first rite is to utter the word "Vaheguru" which is the Gurmantar,[5] to the child. The midwife should ideally be a Sikh, so that she can enact this rite. If the midwife is a non-Sikh then the child's parents or family should state the Gurmantar so that it is the first thing that the newborn hears.

Amrit is to be prepared immediately after the birth of the child. This is to be done as soon after the birth as possible and can be prepared at the place of birth, in the following way:

- An Ardas (prayer of supplication) is performed before the start of the ceremony
- An Amritdharee[6] Singh should get a Sarab Loh[7] bowl and half fill it with water.
- Five patase[8] should be added to the water

---

[5] Blessed word of the Guru – this is the word that is to be meditated upon at all times and leads to emancipation.
[6] Initiated Sikh
[7] Pure iron
[8] Sugar puffs made of sugar and glucose. More than five patase can be added depending on the size of the patase and the utensils used.

- This mixture is to be continuously stirred with a Sarbloh Kirpan[9]
- During the stirring of the 'Amrit' (water & patase), the Singh performing the birth ceremony is to recite Japji Sahib from memory and is to sit in the 'Bir-Asan' position, a Warrior stance[10]
- Once the Japji Sahib recital is complete the Amrit is ready and an Ardas is to be performed and then the Amrit can be administered.

Five drops from the tip of the Kirpan are to be dropped carefully into the mouth of the newborn child and the mother is to drink the rest of the Amrit. This is the first ceremony of initiation of a child into the Khalsa Panth (Sikh Nation).

The mother can then proceed to breast-feed the child (so the first thing that the newborn consumes is Amrit), from this the child should become virtuous, a warrior, saintly, charitable and a vibrant Gursikh. Enacting any other sort of other birth rites/ceremony is not allowed in Sikhi; for example lucky charms or strings tied on the child's wrist or around their neck. To break all superstitions a Sarab Loh Kara is to be placed on the child's right-hand wrist. Drinking alcohol and eating meat whilst celebrating the birth of a child is a grave sin.

After the above ceremony[11], Karah Parshad is to be prepared and an Ardas recited in the presence of Sri Guru Granth Sahib

---

[9] Blessed sword

[10] The left leg is to be folded inwardly to rest on and the right is to be upright, similar to a sprinters stance before a race

[11] Taking the newborn child into the presence of Sri Guru Granth Sahib to be blessed and named are to be done as soon as is physically possible, but superstitions of the mother not going to the Gurdwara for 40 days are not to be adhered to.

Jee.   The child's name is based on the first letter of the Hukamnama[12] taken from Sri Guru Granth Sahib Jee.

If possible on the same day a Sehaj Paath[13] should be started. The child and their mother should listen to the whole Paath. At the Bhog (completions of recital) Guru ka Langar[14] is to be served to the Sadh Sangat (Holy Congregation).

---

[12] Command of the Guru
[13] A complete recital of Sri Guru Granth Sahib Jee, which is completed at intervals
[14] Blessed Free food, this is served at Gurdwaras throughout the world in all services and ceremonies.

2) EDUCATION CEREMONY/ VIDIYA SANSKAR (second ceremony)

"By Guru's Grace, contemplate spiritual knowledge;
read it, study it, and you shall be honored."
(SGGSJ Ang 1329)

It is essential that the child's parents ensure that the child is educated. Those parents who do not educate their offspring are like enemies to them.

"Those parents who say 'I have a lot of virtues and knowledge' and then do not educate their children, are on a par to enemies to them. These parents don't gain any status, their children don't gain any knowledge, this has been proven in the world."
(Sri Guru Nanak Parkash, First half, 6, Vol.2, p.172)

When the child reaches the appropriate age they should be enrolled at a school where they can maintain the Sikh lifestyle and improve their Sikhi discipline. When choosing educational induction for children their spiritual advancement should be the driving factor for choice of school, college and university.

There are two types of education, one is worldly and the other is spiritual. Wordly knowledge alone, without knowledge of God is useless, tasteless and of no benefit. It does not make this human birth worthwhile; rather, it creates ego and atheism, trapping the individual in the reincarnation cycle of births and deaths.

The Gurmukhi[15] language – Gurbani, is to be taught to the child by gaining the guidance of a committed and faithful Gursikh.

---

[15] This is the language created by the Sikh Gurus and has many dialects within it which are expressed in Gurbani, the hymnd of the Sikh Guru's. It is not

4

*"Oh brother the Gurmukhi language should be
taught to a Sikh by another Sikh."*
(Rehatnama Bhai Dhesa Singh Jee)

The child is not to be taught Gurbani or the philosophy of
the Guru, by a non-Amritdharee[16] or a non-believer of the Guru.
A child taught by a Gursikh who has complete faith in Guru
Sahib will have Gurmat[17] enshrined in them. The child is to be
kept away from bad or sinful company who behave in un-Sikh,
un-Godly ways, for example watching corrupting
films/programmes, listening to shameful music, playing cards[18],
gambling, foul language and stealing.

*"Sikh Husband and Wife congregate
and discuss the boundless God.
Teaching their children how to meditate,
And repeatedly praise the Lord."*
(Rehatnama Bhai Sahib Singh Jee, p.160)

Mothers are to maintain a strong level of Sikh discipline.
Daily after their Nitnem (prayer recitals) they should go to the
Gurdwara Sahib[19], listen to discourses of Gurmat, Sikh History
and Kirtan, taking their young children with them. The
experiences of childhood become engraved on the child like a
carving on a stone.

These childhood experiences will become a foundation
for the rest of their lives. If a child becomes religious at a young

---

confined within the grammar of the Panjabi language and has it's own
semantics and syntax.
[16] One who has not been initiated into the fold of Sikhi by taking Amrit
[17] Knowledge of the Sikh Gurus
[18] An activity which just wastes time which could be spent on more
productive activities
[19] Name of Sikh Place of Worship

age then they will become spiritual, charitable, saintly and a warrior. During childhood the child should be educated about the Sikh Gurus, the Great Martyrs, the Great Sikhs and Saints; they will thus grow up virtuous.

3) AMRIT[20] CEREMONY / AMRIT SANSKAR (third ceremony)

Amrit is a blessing of the Guru that makes the individual immortal and breaks the cycle of birth and deaths.

"Drink Amrit, live forever.
Attain extreme bliss by meditating on God."
(SGGSJ Ang 496)

Satguru by creating sweet Amrit and Karah Parshad[21] has blessed us greatly. By blessing us with Amrit of the Khanda[22], Guru Sahib has enshrined a new way of life for humanity.

"To resolve the dispute of the four ages men and women
have been given the one treasure of Naam."
(SGGSJ Ang 797)

Differences in caste, creed, colour, gender, rich and poor all have been eliminated by the creation of the Khalsa.[23] The true Guru is all powerful,

---

[20] Immortal Nectar

[21] Sweet Blessed Food, which is made of flour, water, sugar and butter. It is prepared for all Sikh ceremonies and services at the Gurdwara, commonly distributed after being blessed at the end of a service or ceremony.

[22] Khanda is a double edged sword, Amrit before the creation of the modern day ceremony was given to initiates by the Guru passing water over His feet and the initiate had to drink this water to become a Sikh. Modern day Amrit is administered by Panj Pyare/Five Beloved Sikhs as was ordained by the 10th Sikh Guru, Sri Guru Gobind Singh Jee on Vaisakhi 1699 AD.

[23] Khalsa = the Pure. One enters the Khalsa fold by taking Amrit and becomes a true Khalsa when he/she becomes the living image of the Guru by becoming knowledgeable and spiritually gifted.

*"My True Guru has the power to
kill and revive the dead."*
(SGGSJ Ang 1142)

In accordance with this Sahib Sri Guru Gobind
Singh Jee beheaded the Panj Pyare (The Five Beloved
Ones) and then brought them back to life with his spiritual
powers. Out of the same iron bowl the Panj Pyare drank the
Amrit, and Guru Jee also requested to be initiated with the
very same Amrit which he had just bestowed[24], thus
becoming initiated into the Khalsa Panth.

*"The wonderful man who is beyond human description,
A great warrior with no match, was revealed.
Wonderful, Wonderful is Guru Gobind Singh
who became Guru and Sikh."*
(Bhai Gurdas Jee, Var. 41)

For future generations, it was established that only
'Panj Pyare' can bestow Amrit and bless the individual
with Gurmantar. Thus, no one individual, can ever perform
the Amrit ceremony on his own and without taking Amrit
one cannot regard him/herself as a Sikh of the Guru[25].
Even mentioning the name of a Guru–less person is sinful,

*"Without the True Guru, there is no Guru at all;
Even the name of a Guruless person is accursed."*
(SGGSJ Ang 435)

When a child reaches the age when they can abide
by the Rehat Maryada they must take Amrit from Panj

---

[24] The Guru thus took Amrit himself and said all should become
initiated by Panj Pyare in the future, so he gave Panj Pyare the
authority of the Guru.
[25] As they have not confirmed their faith

8

Pyare. Importantly, before taking Amrit, every person should remember that once initiated, they must only marry an individual that is Amritdharee. It is the individual's responsibility that this is done. If the person is of a young age, then the parents or close family members must accept this responsibility of marriage to another Amritdharee.

If a married person takes Amrit by themselves and their spouse is not Amritdharee, then they can not have a physical relationship with them unless they too become Amritdharee. Just as a clean dish coming into contact with an unclean one also becomes dirty, the same is true for a married couple (where only one spouse is Amritdharee). A husband and wife should take Amrit together in order for them to maintain their Rehat. A married person does not have permission to take Amrit without their spouse, but if they insist upon taking Amrit they must abide by the above conditions.

3.1) The Provision of Amrit & the selection of the Panj Pyare

The Singh's (Panj Pyare) bestowing the Amrit should be of the highest discipline, true Khalsa. One Singh is to be the Pehradaar (guardsman at the door where the Amrit Sanchar is taking place). Two highly disciplined Singh's should prepare Karah Parshad and bring it into the presence of Sri Guru Granth Sahib Jee and then recite Anand Sahib[26] (the whole 40 verses). All the instruments for the ceremony have to be of Sarab Loh, for example the bowls, bucket, vessel, cauldron, spatula, Khanda and a large Kirpan. A stone mortar is to be used to place the Bata upon to prepare the Amrit. All the items are to be cleaned

---

[26] A prayer of bliss which was revealed by the 3rd Guru, Sri Guru Amar Das Jee

with sand prior to their use. The Panj Pyare and Granthi Singh are to also clean their Kirpans and Karas with sand and then wash their Gatras[27]; they are to have a full bath from head to toe prior to the ceremony (including washing their hair) and to wear fresh clothes for the ceremony. They are also to have Panj Ishnana (wash their hands, feet, and face) directly before entering the Darbar of Sri Guru Granth Sahib Jee. Those who do the seva of Panj Pyare are to be of high morality and spirituality, very disciplined in every aspect of life.

Bhai Choupa Singh Jee writes in a Rehatnama that a Sikh should "take Amrit and not partake in any other form of religious initiation. The Sikh is to take initiation from those that are very spiritual and moralistic. The Panj Pyare are not to be one-eyed, bald, lepers, beardless, of bad habits, be thieves or gamblers and not entangled in vice. From those that we get initiated from – we take some of their virtues as this is what they invest in the Amrit, which is why someone of high Sikhi discipline is to be sought to get initiated from."

The Panj Pyare and the Granthi Singh are to all wear the same colour clothes and these should be from the following colours, saffron, blue or white. Their Kirpans are to be worn over their clothes, a Kamar-Kasa (waistband) is to be tied and a parna (scarf like cloth) is to be placed around their neck before entering the Darbar. Their Gatra's are not to be of leather. The Pehradaar is to be a highly disciplined Sikh. The five Singh's[28] are to humbly bow to Sri Guru Granth Sahib Jee and stand up, the sixth Singh is to do the same and stand holding his hands together. The Jathedar is to hold a large Sri Sahib (3 foot

---

[27] Kirpan holster
[28] Singh = Lion, male Sikh's surname

10

kirpan) in his right hand and do the Chaur Sahib Seva[29] with his left. He is to question the sixth Singh – "Are you a highly disciplined Sikh? Do you keep the discipline of the 5 Kakkaars? Have you committed any of the four cardinal sins? Do you recite the specified daily Nitnem prayers? If the Singh is married, he is to be asked if his spouse is living in accordance with the Rehat Maryada. The Singh is to face Sri Guru Granth Sahib Jee and reply humbly that with the Guru Jee's blessing I am living according to the Rehat Maryada. I have not committed any cardinal sin and recite the daily Nitnem prayers. I am physically complete, fit and healthy. He should say that he is forever erroneous due to the entrapments of the mind (showing his humility). If he is married, then he should say that his wife is also a highly disciplined Sikh and lives by the Rehat Maryada. The Jathedar is to question all the six Singh's individually, moving from his right to his left. After the questioning is over – if all are suitable, one Singh becomes the Granthi Singh and the rest join the Jathedar in becoming Panj Pyare.

NB: Those taking part in the seva of Panj Pyare must know all the five prayers from memory. A Jakara (war cry) is only to be sounded on the last Ardas (supplication prayer) of the ceremony.

3.2) Ardas for the worthiness of the Amrit Ceremony Sevadars

The Panj Pyare are to then stand in front of Sri Guru Granth Sahib Jee and perform the following Ardas, "True Guru, Great King, questioning of the Panj Pyare and

---

[29] Chaur Sahib = Whisk that is reverently waved over Sri Guru Granth Sahib, a mark of it's Kingly status

the Granthi Singh have been performed, please forgive us for our shortcomings, make us worthy to prepare Amrit."

3.3) Questioning of initiates

The initiates are to enter the Darbar one by one. They must have fully bathed (including washed hair), wearing - clean simple clothes, the five Kakkaars and a Kirpan with a gatra worn over their clothes. If married, then the Singh and Singhni must come together. All initiates are to bow to Guru Sahib, rise and bring together their hands. If a couple - the Singh is to stand on the right hand-side and the Singhni on the left hand-side. The Jathedar[30] of the Panj Pyare with a drawn Sri Sahib (large sword) in his right hand should ask the initiates why they have come to the ceremony. The initiates with both hands together should reply that they have come to take Amrit, 'bless us with the gift of Amrit.' The Jathedar is to then ask, will you live according to the Rehat Maryada. The initiates are to reply with humility that with the grace of the Guru that they will be able to achieve this.

The Jathedar is to say that they must consider their mind, wealth and life as belonging to Guru Jee, always remaining within the practices of the Khalsa nation and never going against the Guru Panth. From this day on, they are to consider their body, mind and wealth as belonging to Satguru Sri Guru Granth Sahib Jee. By earning an honest living, Dasvandh (one tenth of earnings) is to be given to the Guru or charitable causes and life is to be conducted in accordance with the Rehat.

---

[30] In this case the Jathedar is the master of ceremonies, Jathedar also means leader

If someone has come to retake Amrit, the Jathedar is to ask - which cardinal sin(s) they have committed and why they have you come to retake Amrit? The person who has come to retake Amrit must freely admit to their mistakes or sins. The Panj Pyare will then unanimously decide on the punishment. An Ardas for forgiveness will be performed at the end of the ceremony and the person can retake Amrit after the new initiates.

In the presence of the Panj Pyare and Sri Guru Granth Sahib Jee appropriate punishment is ordained for any sins commited, but even the most serious sins are forgiven. The person who comes and begs for forgiveness is not punished in the afterlife in the Court of God and Dharamraj (God's judge in the afterlife) cannot punish that person. If the person does not admit to their sins here, then they will get punished in God's Court and may have to go through various life-forms, births and deaths as punishment. The person that retakes Amrit is to accept the punishment ordained, as being just and act upon it. Until all the punishment has been completed, the person is to consider themselves as sinful and their sins as not having been forgiven. After completing the punishment, Karah Parshad is to be prepared and an Ardas is to be performed. That person can then consider themselves as forgiven and can become one of the Panj Pyare in future Amrit ceremonies.

Those taking Amrit for the first time do not get punished for their past sins/mistakes. It is the duty of each Amritdharee Singh that he gets his Singhni to take Amrit or vice versa. Bhai Choupa Singh Jee Shibar in his explanation of the Rehat (p.117) writes that a Sikh who does not attempt to inspire/educate their spouse to take Amrit are punishable.

All the initiates are to have their beards flowing and not tied up in anyway. Their turbans are to have been tied one layer at a time (not placed on their heads like a hat). The turban is to be saffron, blue, black or white. The male initiates should not be wearing trousers/pyjama, watches or any jewellery. The female initiates are not to have any jewellery on their hands, in their ears/nose and their hair is to be in a bun/top knot and not in plaits, they should maintain this simplicity of dress and attire for the rest of their lives.[31] After the questioning of all the initiates has been completed, they are to stand in the presence of Satguru and the Jathedar then questions all of them collectively:

"Have you all had a full ishnaan (bath) including the washing of hair? Are you all wearing a Kangha, Kirpan, Kara, and Kashera?"

When all the preparations are complete the Jathedar is to tell all the initiates that they must stand up and remain standing until the Amrit is prepared. The initiates are told to listen attentively to the Five Prayers and are to look directly at Sri Guru Granth Sahib Jee, concentrating their vision upon Sri Guru Granth Sahib Jee. If any of the initiates encounter any serious physical problems whilst standing, then they should sit down. No one is to talk whilst the Amrit is being prepared. The initiates should have love, fear and faith in Guru Sahib, they are about to be blessed with Amrit and the cycle of births and deaths shall end.

---

[31] Sikh women are also to keep their head covered at all times, it is best to wear a small turban. The Guru's command is for both men and women to wear turbans.

3.4)   Ardas to prepare Amrit

In order to maintain purity, the Khanda, the iron bowl and stone-mortar are to be washed thoroughly before use. A woollen blanket is to be laid out, upon which the stone mortar is placed, upon which, the iron bowl with the iron Khanda is positioned. Water from a river/spring, a well or a hand-pump is to be filtered before use and added to the Bata (the iron bowl)[32]. It is essential the area or mouth of the tap, well, or hand pump is washed prior to taking the water for Amrit ceremony. Similarly, Patase are to be fresh and checked for dirt or any imperfections before they are brought into the presence of Sri Guru Granth Sahib Jee.

The Panj Pyare then perform Ardas, "True King, the Panj Pyare stand in your presence in order to prepare Amrit da Bata[33]. As per your order, you will be present in the Panj Pyare. We beg you to bless us with perfect concentration and pronunciation whilst reciting the Five Prayers. Bless us so we may be able to bestow Amrit upon those gathered here today."

3.5)   Preparing Amrit

After the Ardas the Granthi Singh is to take a Hukamnama from Sri Guru Granth Sahib Jee, and the initiates are to remain standing after bowing. The initiates are to fix their sight upon Guru Sahib and listen attentively to the Gurbani being uttered, with their hands clasped together. They are not to talk or wander about.

---

[32] The water is filtered by the Panj Pyare holding a clean piece of cloth over the bata and pouring the water through it.
[33] Bowl of Amrit

The Panj Pyare are to form a circle around the Bata and take up the Bir Asan position. The Panj Payre will add Patase to the water in the bata turn by turn.

The Panj Payre are to start from the right-hand side of Guru Sahib Jee and pass the Khanda from one to the other. It is to be held with four fingers clasped with the thumb at the top. In the left hand a large Sri Sahib[34] is to be held, the tip of which is to be rested upon the shoulder and the handle rested on the edge of the bata. Before commencing to recite Gurbani, the Granthi Singh is told to fix his sight upon the bata and to mentally follow the prayers being recited. The first Singh will concentrate on the bata and begin reciting the Japji Sahib from memory, in a loud clear voice. He is to continually stir the Khanda in the bata simultaneously as he recites Japji Sahib. The other four Pyare are to place both their hands upon the bata, they too will mentally recite the Gurbani that is being read and concentrate on the bata. Upon completion of Japji Sahib, all are to respectively bow their heads and utter the 'Fateh'.[35]

When the Khanda is passed to the second Singh, it is to be kept in the Amrit and is to be passed to his hand. The Kirpan is also to be passed in the same way, maintaining complete contact with the bata at all times. The second Singh reads Jaap Sahib, the third reads Tvaeparsad Svaye, the fourth Singh reads Kabyo Bach Benti Choupai (27 verses), Svaya and Dohra. The fifth Singh recites all forty verses of Anand Sahib. After the complete recitation of each prayer, the 'Fateh' is uttered. Whilst Gurbani is being recited no one is to utter a single

---

[34] Sword
[35] The Sikh greeting which translates to – The Khalsa belongs to the wonderful enlightener (God) as do all victories.

word, they must not allow their eyes to wander around and through the whole ceremony must remain fully alert.

The eyes of the Panj Pyare looking into the Bata of Amrit are considered to be the ten eye's of the Ten Gurus looking into the Bata of Amrit. The placing of the hands of the Panj Pyare on the bata also have the same significance, as the hand's of the Gurus being placed upon the bata of Amrit.

3.6) Ardas for the completion of the preparation of the Amrit

Once the Amrit has been prepared, the Panj Pyare are to lift the bata upon their hands and stand up. The Jathedar is to carry on stirring the Khanda in the Amrit and perform Ardas, "True King with your blessing Panj Pyare have recited Five Prayers and created Amrit. Whilst reciting the prayers and preparing Amrit many mistakes could have been made, please bless us and forgive our faults. In the Amrit is vested your unlimited spiritual power, please free those who become initiated, from the cycle of births & deaths and assist them in upholding their Rehat, bless them with Gursikhi." After the Ardas has been performed the bata is to be placed upon the stone-mortar. A covering is to be placed over the bata and held by the Panj Pyare and the initiates told to be seated. The Granthi Singh then takes a Hukamnama.

3.7) Bestowing Amrit

After listening to the Hukamnama a blanket is placed on a table, upon which the stone-mortar and the bata of Amrit are placed. Two smaller iron bata's are placed on the floor. Men and women are separated and turn by turn each person steps forward. They will sit in 'Bir Asan' and place their right palm over their left to receive Amrit in their hands. The Pyara bestowing the Amrit is to place a handful of Amrit into the hands of the initiate, who is to drink it with true love. At this point the Pyara bestowing the Amrit is to say "Utter – Vaheguru Jee Ka Khalsa, Vaheguru Jee Kee Fateh" the initiate is to reply "Vaheguru Jee Ka Khalsa, Vaheguru Jee Kee Fateh." The initiate is not to say "Sri" during the Fateh nor are they to say "Utter/Bol." In this manner the Pyara bestowing the Amrit is to place five cupped handfuls of Amrit into the hands to be drunk. He bestows Amrit five times in the eyes and five droplets into the Kes of each initiate and the Gurfateh is to be uttered as mentioned above for each time that Amrit is given to the initiate.

> *"The Sikh takes Amrit of the Pahul (iron bowl)*
> *To become initiated.*
> *According to the code of conduct.*
> *Five cupped handfuls are placed in the mouth,*
> *Five in the head and five in the eyes ..."*
> (Rehatnama Bhai Choupa Singh Jee, Shibar, p.91)

After taking Amrit, each person is to respectfully bow to Sri Guru Granth Sahib Jee and utter Gurfateh to all the Sangat. When everyone has taken Amrit, they all must stand up in a line. Two Pyare will hold the bata in their hands and the initiates will in turn place both their hands on the bata and take two mouthfuls of Amrit each. If there is still Amrit left then this should be further shared out between the initiates. **NB:** If there are many initiates then more than two iron bata's can be placed on the floor when administering Amrit (so that more than two people at a time can be initiated).

If an Amritdharee has committed a minor mistake then they should be given appropriate punishment and Choola (a handful of Amrit) is to be given. Punishment can be washing dishes, cleaning shoes, doing seva in the Langar or something of a similar nature. The Panj Pyare can also order the individual to recite Gurbani or meditate for a specific time or length as a punishment for their mistake/sin. An Amritdharee's children should be given Choola[36] and they are not to eat from the same plate as non-Amritdharees and are to be brought up to be Sikhs and taught to abstain from commiting cardinal sins.

3.8) Mool Mantar[37] and the manifestation of Gurmantar in the initiates

In the presence of Sri Guru Granth Sahib Jee the Panj Pyare then make all the Singhs and Singhni's stand and collectively repeat the Mool Mantar five times, investing all its spiritual powers into the initiates.

God is One, without opposition. He is the Creator.
True is His Name
The doer of all that is manifest
He is without fear. He is without enmity
Timeless is His form
Beyond Births and Deaths
Self-Existent
Realised by the grace of the Guru
Meditate on this Name

---

[36] The Choola is only administered to prepare children to take Amrit in the future. Choola is not administered at the end of the Amrit Sanchar to Sangat from outside of the Amrit Sanchar, it is only given to children who are too young to take Amrit or to Amritdharees who have commited a minor discrepancy.
[37] This is the root teaching of Sikhi and is the first utterance in Sri Japji Sahib

True before the Ages. True at the start of the Ages
True now. Sri Guru Nanak Dev Jee says, He shall be true
in the future.

In the same manner, Vaheguru (Gurmantar) is to be repeated five times and in the same way all its powers become invested in the individual, by repeating it in the presence of Guru Sahib. They are to utter the Gurfateh after this.

> *"Vaheguru is Gurmantar*
> *by meditating upon it ego is erased."*
> (Bhai Gurdas Jee, Var. 13)

After this, one of the Panj Pyare will then tell the initiates what the Rehat Maryada is, which has been the same since the formation of the Khalsa. Only the Panj Pyare have the right to announce the Maryada[38]. After this, all stand and perform Ardas for Karah Parshad and have become initiated into the Khalsa Panth.

In the Ardas the Jathedar then utters:

"Maharaj Jee! Whilst creating the Amrit, bestowing it, investing the Mool Mantar and Gurmantar, narrating the Rehat Maryada, giving out punishment, we must have made many mistakes, please forgive our faults. Please bless us with true knowledge in the future. Free the

---

[38] Whilst the Jathedar is announcing the Rehat, 3 Anand Sahibs are to be mentally recited, one Singh out of the Panj Pyare can recite all three paats or three Singhs including the Granthi can recite one Paath each. To fulfil any great supplication to the Guru, if three Anand Sahibs are recited followed by an Ardas by Panj Singh the fete will be accomplished. In this example of the Amrit Sanskar, the Anand Sahibs are recited to forgive the initiates of their past sins and supplicate they maintain their rehat.

initiates from the cycle of births and deaths, and keep them within your Rehat Maryada."

After the Ardas, a Hukamnama is taken from Sri Guru Granth Sahib Jee. Any initiate who has not had their names based upon a Hukamnama from Guru Jee, must take new names from the first letter of the Hukamnama. Karah Parshad is then distributed to end the ceremony.

NB: If someone's wedding has not been performed according to Gurmat, i.e. an Anand Karaj has not been performed, that Singh and Singhni are to get married according to Gurmat before the final Ardas of the ceremony. Anand Sahib is to be recited followed by an Ardas.

3.9) Teachings given by the Panj Pyare

"It is by the offering of your head that the Five Singhs administer Amrit and you receive the boon of Amrit. The five narrate a discipline, which is to be thought of at all times and never forgotten."
(Rehatnama Bhai Desa Singh Jee)

The Jathedar of the Panj Pyare is to utter the Fateh, as is the tradition from Satguru's time, and congratulate the 'new' initiates. He also says, "Khalsa Jee, many of you are blessed for on this day you have received Satguru Jee's gift of Amrit. You have shaken off the influence of Guruless people. You now belong to the Guru. From this day forward, you are the sons and daughters of the Guru, and your mind, body and wealth belong to the Guru. Having taken the Guru's Amrit, your previous caste, family name and sins are no more. Your previous life is finished and today you have taken birth in the House of the Guru. You are all now part of the Khalsa family:

21

- Your Spiritual Father is Sahib Sri Guru Gobind Singh Jee;

- Your Spiritual Mother is Mata Sahib Kaur Jee;

- Your Place of Birth is Takhat Sri Kesgarh Sahib, Sri Anandpur Sahib;

- Your Maternal home (Nanakee) is Guru Ka Lahore;

- Your Obedience is to the One Timeless Lord;

- Your only Guru is Sri Guru Granth Sahib Jee.

- You are not to bow or obey any other as your Guru;

- Your examination is only via the Shabad and Gurbani;

"The Shabad is the Guru and it is to be worshipped.
It is very deep and unfathomable,
The people of the world would be insane,
without this Shabad."
(SGGSJ Ang 635)

Your Vision is of the Khalsa:

"Where five Singhs with excellent rehat are congregated,
See my true form/spirit within them."

"The Khalsa - an Amritdharee disciplined
Sikh is my true form,
I am present in such Sikhs."

Your Worship is of Akaal Purkh (the Timeless Lord).

22

By living according to the Rehat, Guru Sahib will bless the individual and the Jathedar says,

"Through the teachings of the True Guru
and birth in the house of the True Guru,
the cycle of births and deaths has been abolished."
(SGGSJ Ang 940)

The Mool Mantar and Gurmantar which have been invested in each individual by the Panj Pyare are to be meditated on at all times, whilst walking, standing, sitting, travelling or working.

In the same way that the Panj Pyare recited the five prayers to prepare the Amrit, those initiated are to recite the five prayers on a daily basis after rising early and having ishnaan (bathing during which meditation is done). In the evening Rehras Sahib is recited and before going to sleep Kirtan Sohela is read. As a minimum these seven prayers must be recited daily by all Amritdharees.

The prayers for Amrit Vela/Ambrosial hours (before dawn) are as follows:

1) **Sri Japji Sahib** – read to attain Brahm Gyan (wisdom of God);

2) **Sri Jaap Sahib** – a salutation to the Timeless Lord and a description of His qualities;

3) **Ten Svaye** – ("Sravag sudh ...") The Svaye are read to attain worldly detachment and abolish false practices;

4) **Sri Chaupai Sahib** – this is recited for protection, having 29 verses in the numerical order as in Sri Dasam Granth Sahib. The recital is to be read up to,

"In the month of Phadro, eight days after Masaya on a Sunday, whilst sitting on the riverside of the Satluj I completed Sri Dasam Granth."
(Dasam Granth Ang 1388)

The Svaya and Dohra are to be recited to complete the prayer;

5) **Sri Anand Sahib** – this recital is for liberation from the cycle of births & deaths and the attainment of Anand (Bliss). **All 40 verses are to be recited;**

6) **Rehras Sahib**[39] – recited so that one does not have to leave Sach Khand (highest spiritual plane);

7) **Kirtan Sohela** – Panj Ishnana (washing feet, hands and face) is performed before going to sleep. After this, one is to sit upon their bed cross-legged, facing their pillow and recite the prayer. Satguru is with us at all times and protects us from the Angel of Death and demons. If one unexpectedly dies in their sleep, they will not enter lower lifeforms. Bad thoughts/dreams do not occur if Kirtan Sohela has been recited. Satguru places an iron fortress around the Sikh so nothing can hurt or scare them.

---

[39] The full Rehras Sahib is to be recited which can be found in Shaheed Bhai Mani Singh's Panj Granthi Pothi, this is the historical proof we have of the Rehras being this length during the times of the Gurus, as Bhai Mani Singh was a contemporary of Guru Sahib. This is the Rehras Sahib that is in the Gutka Sahibs of Damdami Taksal

3.10) Five Kakkaars

After being initiated a Sikh is to never remove any of the five Kakkaars from their body.

The following five K's are the mark of Sikhi. These five can never be parted from the body. Kara, Kirpan, Kashera, Kangha, recognise these as four of them. The fifth is Kesh, without which the other four are useless. There are also four H's which must be avoided. Understand this without any doubt, no lies have been told. Hukka, taking tobacco(including any other type of intoxicants). Hajamat - removing/cutting of hair. Halalo - eating meat. Haram - adultery (sexual relationships outside of marriage). These are the four H's. Dyeing of beards (including any other bodyily hair) and the wearing of mehndi (including other types of make up) is strictly forbidden. (Asfokat Svaye, Sri Dasam Granth)

1.Kesh – Unshorn Hair

From your head down to your toes all hair is to be kept unshorn and your hair is to be tied and complemented with a turban,

"...complete form is with turban donned."
(SGGSJ Ang 1084)

For the respect of your hair, two turbans are to be tied, tying each layer one at a time. There should be a small turban tied underneath and a larger one tied above this. Women must not plait their hair[40] and should keep their hair tied in a bun/top-knot, in order to respect your

---

[40] Plaiting of the hair is forbidden as it is viewed as styling your hair, all types of hairstyle are forbidden and the hair should be simply tied and complemented with a turban.

Kesh a small turban should be tied. Keski is not a kakkar (one of the five K's).

"Sri Guru Gobind Singh Jee says,
listen to this command oh beloved,
This is the essential pre-requisite to attain my darshan.
Without arms and kesh I will not give you darshan."

God also revealed Himself as Kesdhari when He gave Darshan/revealed Himself to Sahib Sri Guru Nanak Dev Jee, He did so in the form of a human with unshorn hair;

"Your nose is so graceful, and your hair is so long."
(SGGSJ Ang 567)

"God does not need to eat; His Hair is Wondrous
and Beautiful; He is free of hate."
(SGGSJ Ang 98)

2. Kangha – Wooden Comb

In order to keep the kesh clean a wooden kangha (Sikh Comb) is to be kept in the hair. According to scientific research keeping a wooden kangha in your hair reduces the level of static energy build up. A metal or ivory comb is not to be used as a substitute.

"Comb the hair twice a day, covering it with a turban that is to be tied from fresh (ie. no folds already put in it). Teeth are to be cleansed with a twig of walnut bark daily (brushed if this is not possible) – thus ill health will be avoided Bhai Nand Lal Jee." (Tankhanama Bhai Nand Lal Jee, p.57)

To keep the hair clean it must be combed twice daily. In the morning and evening after combing your hair a turban is to be tied. It is to be tied a layer at a time, and it is to be removed in the same manner, taking it off a layer at a time. Starch and pins are not to be added to the turban, which would make it look like a hat.

> *"Being a Sikh he/she who wears a hat –*
> *will enter into seven diseased life forms."*
> (Rehatnama Bhai Prehlad Singh Jee, p.65)

If your kangha becomes damaged in anyway it should be replaced immediately. The kangha is placed on the head, the highest point of the body and thus becomes supreme. In the same way the Khalsa is to become supreme by removing ego and being humble. Just as the kangha removes broken hairs and cleans the hair physically, it is also spiritually questioning the individual as to how many good and bad deeds have been committed during the day. Just as clean hair is attached to your head so are your good deeds. Similarly, as broken hairs are removed by your kangha, your vices should be removed in the same way. The hairs removed by the kangha are not to be thrown in a dirty place or on the floor. They are to be kept in a clean and container and when enough hair has gathered they are to be burnt, this is out of respect for the Kes which are worth more to a Sikh than their own life. The ashes of the Kes are then to be dispersed in flowing natural water (stream, river or ocean). Women and children are to tie a string to their kangha so that it can easily be tied to their hair, and to stop it from falling. Approximately four spare kanghas should be kept at home.

3. Kara – iron bracelet

The Kara must be of Sarab Loh (pure iron). The Khalsa is not to wear a kara that is made of gold, silver, brass, copper or one that has grooves in it[41]. Only the Sarab Loh Kara is acceptable to Guru Jee. The Kara is a handcuff placed by the Guru upon the individual to remind us of our duty to God, stopping us from committing sins. The Kara acts as a defence if someone goes to strike you with a sword on your wrist. According to scientific research, the Kara adds to the iron levels in the body by rubbing on the skin. The Kara teaches us that these arms belong to Sahib Sri Guru Gobind Singh Jee – with which we are not to steel, con, commit forgery, oppress, bully, persecute, sin or murder. Gambling and playing cards are not permitted.

With our hands we should earn an honest living and share its benefits. In addition, your hands should serve your community and the Khalsa nation. The Kara is a precious gift bestowed upon us for life by Guru Sahib, which cannot be separated from the body. The Kara is circular having no beginning and no end, similarly God has no beginning or end and the Kara reminds us of this.

---

[41] The Kara must be circular and with no grooves in it as it signifies God's eternal power, the grooves would mean this power has breaks in it and the symbolic reminder of the Kara is lost. Also some purchase these grooved Karas to act as a weapon, but the Kara is not a weapon, Maharaj has blessed us with a Kirpan for battle purposes. The Kara must also be wide with at least a few millimetres of width, thus it must not be a mere Chakkar (round thin circle).

4. Kirpan – Sword of Mercy

"The mark of a Khalsa
is one who holds a Kirpan in hand,
by wearing the Kirpan millions of sins are abolished."[42]
(Sri Dasam Granth, Ang 42)

The Kirpan is there to protect the poor and for self-defence. With patience and mercy, the Kirpan is to be used as a sword to destroy oppression. The Kirpan is to always be in a gatra and never to be removed from the body. The Kirpan protects us from hidden and seen enemies. The Kirpan is a weapon to protect the whole body, as a minimum it should be nine inches in length.[43] Keeping the Kirpan in a Kangha[44], in the Kesh and putting it on a string around the neck like a Janeoo, are against the Rehat and forbidden.

"Those who never depart with their arms,
they are the Khalsa with excellent conduct."
(Rehatnama Bhai Desa Singh Jee, p.148)

You are never to walk over your Kirpan or other weapons. When washing your Kesh, the Kangha is to be tied to your Kirpan and the Kirpan tied around your

---

[42] Millions of sins are abolished by the Kirpan acting as a constant physical and spiritual reminder of the teachings of the Guru.
[43] This length is suggested as the Kirpan needs to be a weapon that can be used. Some Sikhs wear very small Kirpans which could not be used to defend others appropriately – the wearer of the Kirpan should be able to fit their hand comfortably onto the handle of the Kirpan in order to grip it firmly.
[44] Some wear a Kangha with a symbolic Kirpan engraved in it, this is not a Kirpan and does not represent the Kirpan as a Kakkar, as it cannot be used as a Kirpan.

29

waist[45]. When bathing, your Kirpan is to be tied around your head (after washing your Kesh) and not tucked into the Kashara as this dishonours your Kirpan. When women bathe they are to tie their dupata or dastar on their head and then their Kirpan. When going to sleep your Kirpan is not to be removed from your body.

The Kirpan is only to be used for two things. Firstly, to give Guru Jee's blessing to freshly prepared Karah Prasad or for langar. Secondly, in order to destroy tyrants and oppressors. It must never be used for anything else.

If the Kangha, Kara or Kirpan are separated from your body, you are forbidden to eat or drink until they are replaced. Upon the replacement of your missing Kakkar, Japji Sahib is to be recited and an Ardas must be performed for the seperation and to beg for forgiveness. The Ardas may be performed either in a Gurdwara or the place where you are replacing your Kakkar. Having done this, you may eat and drink.

5. Kashera – Long shorts

The Kashera is underwear blessed to us by the Guru, it is white in colour and looks like a long pair of shorts.

"The sign of true chastity is the Kashera you must wear this, and hold weapons in hand."
(Bhai Gurdas Jee, Var. 41, pauri 15)

---

[45] You can wrap your small dastar around your waist to assist holding the Kangha & Kirpan in place when washing your Kesh

The Kashera is the sign of sexual restraint and a constant reminder of our moral duties as Sikhs. The Kashera and Kirpan are never to be separated from the body.

"The Kashera and Kirpan are never to leave the body."
(Rehatnama Bhai Desa Singh Jee p.147)

You are only to wear Rev Kashera (a traditional style Kashera)[46]. The Kashera gives us the teaching,

"Men should look at the opposite sex
as mothers, sisters and daughters,
(women should look at the opposite sex
as fathers, brothers and sons)."
(Var. 29, Pauri 11, Bhai Gurdas Jee)

The Kashera is never to leave your body completely i.e. stepping out of it with both your legs. After doing Ishnaan, one half of the wet Kashera is to be removed from one leg and a dry clean Kashera is to be put on that leg, and similarly for the other leg. If the Kashera does leave the body by accident, then you are to approach "Five Singhs" who will do Ardas for you and give you a punishment.[47] If the Kangha, Kirpan and Kara leave the body you can do an Ardas yourself, but if the Kashera leaves the body only "Five Singhs" can do the Ardas. The Kashera is never to be changed whilst your head is uncovered.

---

[46] A Rev Kashera is different from normal underwear in that it has brakes on it, in that the Kashera tapers to fit the leg above the knee.
[47] You have to do this upon the Kashera leaving your body and not other Kakkars as the Five Singhs who do your Ardas for forgiveness can question you upon the circumstances of the Kashera leaving your body. As in some cases of moral lapse the person may also have to present themselves at the next available Amrit Sanchar and ask for forgiveness for any moral discretions.

3.11) The Four Cardinal Sins

Hukka Smoking tobacco, and all other intoxicants

Hajamat Cutting, plucking, surgically removing, dying/bleaching hair. Defacing body by piercing or tattooing.

Halaal Eating meat, fish and eggs

Haram Adultery and sexual relationships outside of marriage

1. Hukka (tobacco and all other intoxicants)

"Listen to the discipline of the Gursikh who relinquishes the accompaniment of tobacco, avoiding bodily contact with tobacco as he/she knows that he/she is better off dead than having to touch tobacco."

By using tobacco, all good deeds are destroyed and the person will suffer for a long time in hell. A Gursikh would rather die than touch tobacco. If a Gursikh comes into contact with anything containing tobacco, for example, cigarettes, cigars, paan, charas, pipes, they must wash their hands with soap at least five times[48]. Then they must purify their Kesh, body and clothes by bathing.

"Meat, all forms of intoxicants (including tobacco, ganja/cannabis and alcohol), wearing of hats and doing the pretense of rubbing soil on the body. A Singh with excellent rehat doesn't associate with people who are

---

[48] This is to ensure thorough cleansing and the washing five times is a suggested minimum to ensure cleanliness.

engrossed in these sinful habits." (Rehatnama Bhai Desa Singh Jee, 148)

"Those that consume even a minuscule amount of tobacco are disowned in the afterlife by their ancestors and drinking water from such a person is similar to drinking alcohol. By drinking alcohol seven generations are exterminated and by consuming Bhang/marajuana the body is destroyed. The person who consumes tobacco exterminates one hundred generations and many generations go to hell because of gossiping."
(Sri Gur Partap Suraj, Rit 5, ansoo 29, volume 13)

Therefore in Gurmat the use of tobacco is strictly forbidden and it should not be touched or used even by mistake. Other religions have also forbid the use of tobacco; a Hindu Puran tells Hindus how to restrain from tobacco in the following way:

"The Brahmin that consumes tobacco
is donated charity by others.
Those that give charity to such a person
Go to hell and the Brahmin becomes a pig."
(Skandh Purana, Dh. 52, Salok 52)

The person, who uses tobacco and then gives charity to Brahmins, goes to Rorve Hell and the Brahmin who receives this charity becomes a pig, cleaning dirty drains and going through many hells.

Satguru has made the use of tobacco a cardinal sin. You are not to eat with or marry your children into the families of those that consume, smoke or use tobacco.

2. Hajamat – Cutting, plucking, dying Kesh

Cutting hair is strictly forbidden in Gurmat. From your head down to your toes, no hair is to be plucked, cut, burnt or chemically/surgically removed. Kesh are not to be dyed by any method whatsoever and the plucking of hair is not permitted.[49]

"God made the human form perfect,
but the treacherous has altered it
And made it lose its natural beauty."

"The treacherous has altered the perfect human body,
Making it lose its natural beauty.
He/She will not get acceptance in the court of God
And is an infidel, a dog and is devil like."

Keeping your Kesh is essential. Upon the death of a relative, the deceased's hair is not to be shaved off. The cutting of hair is prohibited in other religions as well, but in Gurmat cutting hair is a cardinal sin and results in a person becoming an outcast. You are to guard against committing this cardinal sin.

Your Kesh are not to be washed with ashes or clay, they are to be washed with shampoo, yoghurt or lasee. Lying down with your Kesh uncovered or partaking in any action with your Kesh uncovered is strictly forbidden. You are not to enter a dusty, dirty place with your Kesh uncovered.

Cutting the Kesh or piercing the ears/noses of your children is strictly forbidden. The hair of children is not to

---

[49] When people start to age they start dying their hair black/brown or plucking their white hairs, this is forbidden and vanity is to be relinquished by enshrining the Guru's teachings

be tied in dreadlocks. From a young age, the Kesh of your children are to be combed with a Kangha.

"The complete form of man is with a beard, which is left untied. The Kesh are combed with a wooden Kangha."

Amritdharee Singhs are to keep their beards open and untied.

3. Halaal – (Kutha/meat)

Kutha meat is meat that is slaughtered in an Islamic way, by torturing the animal and bleeding it to death. A Sikh is to never eat this type of meat and it makes a Sikh an apostate. In Sri Guru Granth Sahib there is no place where permission to eat meat is given on the contrary it is condemned consistently and continually. A person that kills an animal and eats it will be reborn in that life form and have to experience being killed and eaten themselves.

"Kabeer, the eating of lentils (masoor) and rice is excellent. It contains Amrit in the form of salt. Who would cut his own throat, to have meat with his chappati?" (SGGSJ Ang 1374)

The Khalsa is a warrior, not being a Vaishnoo (those who do not kill any other living beings), but at the same time the Khalsa is not a butcher who kills for meat. Guru Jee used to go hunting to free souls from the cycle of births and deaths. We do not have the power to become Mukt (liberated) ourselves from the cycle of births and deaths let alone liberate others. When Sri Guru Nanak Dev Jee lived at Sultanpur, a Qazi (Muslim priest) was killing a chicken but it escaped from his clutches and splashed his clothing with blood. The Qazi said to his servant, my clothes have become dirty, go and fetch fresh clothes.

Satguru Jee composed the following Shabad in reference to the Qazi,

"If blood has stained your clothing you say your clothes have become impure. How can the mind of those who eat meat, drink blood and suck bones become pure?"
(SGGSJ Ang 140)

Qazi! If your clothes have become impure due to bloodstains then how can your mind stay pure after eating a chicken which is so large and full of blood. Eating meat just to satisfy your taste buds is strictly forbidden.

God has created 36 types of vegetarian food for you to consume, by eating meat your intellect becomes like that of an animal. Your mind becomes unwilling to recite Gurbani. Baba Deep Singh Jee lived on a diet of unripe Ber (a tropical fruit) and hand wrote four volumes of Sri Guru Granth Sahib Jee, which were placed at four of the Takhats. At the age of 87, he went to war and defeated the tyrants. Within him he had the power of Naam, Bani and Amrit.

To conclude, eating meat is not allowed in any form, this includes fish and eggs and ingredients in foods with lecithin (egg), egg trace, gelatins etc. The Guru's teachings are more precious to us than the pleasures of our tastebuds, we should try adopting a simple diet and steer away from eating processed foods which do commonly contain ingredients which we cannot consume, if you do consume these foods you must not become lazy or purposely ignorant of the ingredients. Thousands have been martyred to uphold this Rehat. Only in survival circumstances are non lacto-vegetarian items allowed in diet but even then Halal and Kosher meat is outlawed for Sikhs.

4. Haraam – Adultery, sexual relationships outside of marriage

In Gurmat, entering sexual relationships outside of marriage is strictly forbidden for both men and women, thus the question of dating does not even arise. Husband and wife must be physically faithful to one another. People, who allow lust to overcome them, and violate this rule, will go to hell and enter other life forms.

"O sexual desire, you lead the mortals to hell;
You make them wander in reincarnation
through countless species."
(SGGSJ Ang 1358)

Sri Guru Gobind Singh Jee was given the following teaching by his Father Sri Guru Teg Bahadur Jee,

"When I was mature enough, Satguru Sri Guru Teg Bahadur Sahib Jee gave me this teaching: Until the day you take your last breath, you must take this in and never forget it. You must forever respect your wife, You must never go into another women's bed, not even in a dream." (Sri Dasam Granth Ang 842)

"Men should look at the opposite sex
as mothers, sisters and daughters,
(women should look at the opposite sex
as fathers, brothers and sons)."
(Var. 29, Pauri 11, Bhai Gurdas Jee)

"Be faithful to your one wife, see others as your daughters and sisters, (for women you must be faithful to one husband and see others as your sons and brothers)."
(Var. 6, Pauri 8, Bhai Gurdas Jee)

A Singh must look upon his wife as his faithful Singhni and a Singhni should look upon her husband as Parmeshwar (God). (This is in terms of the respective roles of each sex – this point is elaborated upon in the full code of conduct contained in 'Gurbani Paath Darpan.' This is only applicable if the Singh is living to the Khalsa ideals, see page 65 of this publication for further explanation.)

Singhs are to see elder women as their mothers, female peers as sisters and younger females as daughters. In the same manner, women are to see elder men as their fathers, male peers as their brothers and younger males as their sons. Those who have sexual relationships outside of marriage go to hell and in the after-life they will suffer the pain of embracing red-hot iron columns.

"...the hot irons are put around his/her body."
(SGGSJ Ang 546)

In the after-life, these individuals are boiled in cauldrons of hot oil.

"Those who enter sexual relationships outside of marriage shall be taken to hell and boiled in very hot oil."
(SGGSJ Ang 1362)

5. Alcohol

In Gurmat, the drinking of alcohol is strictly forbidden. The word for alcohol is 'Sharaab' which means 'sharaarat' mischief, and 'aab' means water, thus it means mischievous or evil water, which is the root of all sins and evil actions. Sri Guru Amar Das Jee writes about alcohol in the following way,

"One person brings a full bottle, and another fills His cup. Drinking wine, His intelligence departs, and madness enters His mind; He cannot distinguish between His own and others, He is struck down by His Lord and Master. Drinking it, He forgets His Lord and Master, He is punished in the Court of the Lord. Do not drink the false wine at all, if it is in your power." (SGGSJ Ang 554)

"Kabeer Jee says, Those who consume marijuana, meat, tobacco, fish and wine. All pilgrimages, fasts and rituals they follow are of no avail."
(SGGSJ Ang 1377)

An Amritdharee should not even look at alcohol, their mind should not ever falter.

"One who trades in this Amrit/Nectar of Naam, How could He ever love the wine of the world?"
(SGGSJ Ang 360)

By drinking alcohol the intellect is destroyed, God is forsaken and the gem of human life is wasted. Those who have evil thoughts drink alcohol. This makes them more lustful which in turn leads them to hell.

"Guru Jee says by drinking this wine one commits countless sins."
(SGGSJ Ang 553)

In the same way it is stated in the Charitar:

"Firstly he is drinking alcohol, secondly he is young, thirdly he is wealthy. How can he escape sinful actions? Only if God is merciful can one be saved from sin."
(Sri Dasam Granth Ang 1077)

In the Rehatnama's the drinking of alcohol is strictly forbidden,

"The Singh that refrains from the following five actions is considered wise, Sexual relations outside of marriage, gambling, lying, steeling, drinking alcohol."
(Rehatnama Bhai Desa Singh Jee, p.149)

Gursikhs are to drink this sort of intoxicant,

"Make spiritual wisdom your molasses, and meditation your scented flowers; Let good deeds be the herbs. Let devotional faith be the distilling fire, and your love the ceramic cup. Thus the sweet nectar of life is distilled."(SGGSJ Ang 360)

3.12) The Five Takhats (Thrones) of the Khalsa

These Five Gurdwaras have been given reverence as the Five Thrones of the Khalsa Panth.

1. Sri Akaal Takhat Sahib

Founded by the 6th Guru, Sri Guru HarGobind Sahib Jee in Sri Amritsar Sahib. This Gurdwara is the highest temporal point for Sikhs and it is from the Akaal Takhat that political and religious decisions of the Panth have been taken and will be taken in the future.

2. Takhat Sri Patna Sahib (Bihar)
The place of birth of the 10th Guru, Sri Guru Gobind Singh Jee. The 9th Guru, Sri Guru Teg Bahadur Jee said that this should be made a Takhat.

3. Takhat Sri Kesgarh Sahib, Sri Anandpur Sahib

The Khalsa was founded here in 1699 by Sri Guru Gobind Singh Jee.

4. Takhat Sri Damdama Sahib, Sabo Ki Talvandi

This is where Sri Guru Gobind Singh Jee recited the complete Sri Guru Granth Sahib Jee (including the Gurbani of the 9th Guru) from the first Ang right through to the final words on Ang 1430 – Shaheed Bhai Mani Singh Jee was the scribe as Guru Sahib uttered Gurbani. Guru Jee revealed the meanings of Gurbani and established a university to teach it (the Taksal). Damdama Sahib is known as 'Guru ki Kanshi' (the school of the Guru). At this Takhat there is a coin from Sri Guru Gobind Singh Jee's time, upon which Takhat Damdama Sahib is inscribed.

A person who does not accept this to be a Takhat, and instead regards a living person as a Takhat, are considered Manmatee (greatly mistaken and against the teachings of the Guru, following the misgivings of their mind).

5.Takhat Abchal Nagar, Sachkand Sri Hazoor Sahib, Nander (Maharastra)

This is where Sri Guru Granth Sahib Jee was annointed as the Guru for eternity by Sri Guru Gobind Singh Jee, who went to Sach Khand from here. Whenever a Sikh goes to a Takhat for the first time they are to donate a minimum of five rupees and give five rupees for Karah Parshad.

3.13) Four Foundations

These Four Gurdwaras are seen as the Foundations of Faith for Sikhs.

1. Sri Nankana Sahib (Pakistan)
Birthplace of Sri Guru Nanak Dev Jee

2. Sri Amritsar Sahib
Popularly referred to as The Golden Temple, this is the holiest shrine of Sikhs

3. Sri Tarn Taran Sahib
The Guru ferries one across the worldyly ocean at this shrine, the Sarovar[50] is blessed with this boon from the Guru and dispels leprosy.

4. Sri Muktsar Sahib
Historical shrine of where 40 Sikhs who deserted the Guru attained Shaheedi/Martyrdom. They first deserted the Guru in battle due to starvation and low rations, but later came to their senses, begging Sri Guru Gobind Singh Jee for forgiveness and joining him in the ensuing battle.

3.14) The Four Colours of the Khalsa

Blue, Black, White and Saffron

These four colours are to be worn, other colours excite the mind and lure it to vices, and are therefore prohibited. Amritdhari Sikhs are specifically not to wear

---

[50] Water tank in which people bathe

red or green at anytime.[51]   One is to dress humbly, any simple colours can be worn. Amritdhari women are not to wear ear rings, nose-rings, rings, bangles, nail polish, lipstick, bindi, henna, keeping long nails, wearing a saree etc. Piercing of any kind is prohibited.

"The Code of Conduct of Satguru Jee is that one is not to pierce their ears or nose."
(Rehatnama Bhai Deya Singh Jee, p. 78)

Sikhs are not to wear rings, ear-rings and other jewellery, Satguru Jee says:

"Guru Jee says your jewellery is Naam,
Which will be of assistance at your time of death."
(SGGSJ Ang 375)

In the next world only the jewellery of Naam is of assistance, worldly jewellery is of no avail. Amritdhari Sikhs are to abstain from jooth (eating food that has already been eaten by others or is being shared or has cross contamination in it). Food from restaurants is not to be consumed. Fruit should be eaten after it has been washed.

Degrading video films, television, cinema, dances are not to be watched. A Singh is not to wear a blanket around his waist in a traditional doti manner or a turla is not to be left out of the turban, (one strand left out of sequence).

---

[51] This is specifically dark green & dark red – as these colours entice the mind & draw attention to the wearer. Humbling colours of simplicity are allowed.

3.15) Five groups of people who are not to be associated with

The following five groups are not to be associated with as they have betrayed the Guru. The company of these five is to be refrained from as they may also influence us to betray the Guru in the same way that they did.

1. Meene
Satguru Ramdas Jee disowned Prithi Chand[52] and called him Meena for having a needless enmity with Sri Guru Arjan Dev Jee. Prithia's descendants are those who once got a Brahmin to attempt to poison Sri Guru Hargobind Sahib Jee, and sent a midwife with poison on her nipples to feed the young Guru. A snake charmer was also sent by Prithia and was told to release his snake on to Guru Sahib to try and kill him. These evil doers, the descendants of Prithia, are called Meene.

2. Masand
In the name of Satguru, Masands collected money for Kar-Seva of Gurdwaras, but they begun to misuse the money and spend it on themselves. They became evil and started oppressing the Sikh Sangat, doing as they pleased. The tenth Guru freed the Sikh Sangat from these reptiles.

Guru Sahib got hot syrup poured over them and they were burnt alive as punishment for their sins. Bhai Prehlad Singh Jee states in his Rehatnama, "You are not to obey Masands, they will con the Sangat.[53]"

---

[52] Prithi Chand or Prithia as he is commonly referred to, was the eldest son of Sri Guru Ram Das Jee, he developed an enmity with Sri Guru Arjan Dev Jee out of jealousy of not being appointed the Guru.
[53] Modern day masands exist in many guises. So if you know of individuals who are fraudulently representing the Guru and/or stealing donations – you are to break ties with such unscrupulous individuals.

3. Ram Raieeay

Sri Guru Har Rai Sahib Jee's eldest son Ram Rai had needless enmity with the eight and ninth Gurus and appointed his own Masands. He changed a line in Gurbani just to please the Mughal emperor Aurangzeb, changing "soil is of the muslim..." to "soil is of the deceitful..."
Sri Guru Har Rai Jee excommunicated Ram Rai from the house of the Guru because he altered Gurbani. Satguru said:

> *"Those who do not fear*
> *and respect Gurbani are not Sikhs."*
> (Sri Guru Partap Suraj Granth)

No Sikh of the Guru's is to associate with Ram Raieeay, nor is any offering to be made to them. Ramrai was told to leave and just go in the direction in which he was facing and he was told to never return. Ramrai had no children. His followers started to call him 'Guru'. The Khalsa should never trust them.

4. Dhir Maleeay

Dhir Mal, the elder brother of Sri Guru Har Rai Sahib Jee, became an enemy of Guru Jee and during the reign of the Sixth Guru, Sri Guru HarGobind Sahib Jee, he left Kartarpur for Kiratpur Sahib. Once there he set himself up as a 'Guru'. Upon the order of Guru Sahib, the Sikhs seized the 'Chaur' from Dhir Mal and threw him out of Kiratpur. Then again at the time of the ninth Guru, Dheer Mal again set up his own throne at Baba Bakala. He also got Sheehee Masand to try and shoot the Ninth Guru.

Those Sodhis from the Doab's Kartarpur area are Dheer Mal's descendants. It was out of these descendants that Vadbhag Singh was born. During the Sikh rule of the

12 Misls (Khalsa States), the governor of Jalandhar desecrated and burnt 'Tham Sahib' Gurdwara. Vadbhag Singh was Amritdharee, being the first Amritdharee of the Dhir Mal clan. He was scared of the Mughal rulers so he didn't go to inform the Singhs (living in the jungles), nor did he confront the rulers about the desecration of 'Tham Sahib.' At that time, the Singhs learnt he had escaped to the mountains to escape persecution and practice black magic. The Dheer Mal clan is excommunicated and is not to be associated with by the Khalsa.

5. Gangu Shaheeay (and Hindaleeay)

Gangu Shah, a Brahmin, handed over the Small Sahibzade/Princes[54] to the Mughal Governor Vazir Khan, who bricked them alive. The disloyal descendants of this family are not to be associated with by the Khalsa.

The Hindaleeay made alterations to the biography of Sri Guru Nanak Dev Jee and had Sikhs arrested leading to their torture and deaths in jails. The descendants of Shehee Masand were the ones who attempted to shoot the ninth Guru and thus betrayed Him.

If any person out of the above five named groups takes Amrit from the Panj Pyare, lives according to the Rehat, accepts Sri Guru Granth Sahib Jee as their Guru and has full faith in the Guru, they are to be considered a fellow brother/sister of the Khalsa.

---

[54] Sons of Sri Guru Gobind Singh Jee, Baba Zoravar Singh Jee and Baba Fateh Singh Jee

3.16) Five not to be associated with (i.e. not to eat with or marry your children to)

1. Tobacco users
People who smoke or use any form of tobacco (or drugs) are not to be associated with.

2. Female Infanticide
Those who kill their daughters at birth:

"The following are all major sins: Killing a Brahmgyani, killing a cow[55], killing or selling your daughter, and eating from a person who has no moral discipline. Anyone who commits any of these sins has committed thousands of sins. This egotistical individual will be reprimanded thousands of times."
(SGGSJ Ang 1413)

"They who kill their daughters and marry their daughters to those who cut their hair are punishable."
(Rehatnama Bhai Deya Singh Jee)

3. Those who sell their daughters
Those who receive money for the marriage of their daughters and take dowry.

4. Those that cut their hair from their head

---

[55] Killing a Cow is seen as a major sin in the Indian sub-continent and this is the reason for Maharaj using the example of killing a cow, but for Sikhs killing any animal is a major sin.

5. Those who completely shave all their hair from their face and head[56]

A Hukamnama from Sri Akaal Takhat Sahib excommunicated Narakdharees/Fake Nirankaris on 30 June 1978.

Radha Soamis, Namdharis, Noormehlie, Bhaniarawale, Sacha Sodha Vale and other groups whom claim their leaders to be the Guru and do not accept Sri Guru Granth Sahib Jee as the supreme Guru, these groups are not to be associated with, married into or meals taken with them. If they take Amrit from Panj Pyare, keep the Khalsa Rehat and accept Sri Guru Granth Sahib Jee as their Guru then they can be associated with and they are our brothers and sisters.

---

[56] Some may be reading this thinking do I stop speaking to anyone who cuts their hair? The Rehat or discipline outlined here is to guide us – that we should not partake food with these individuals and/or marry our children into their families. We all have to decide our own personal rehat/discipline whilst being practical and non-hypocritical. We must watch our every move and ensure we are not becoming egotistical or hypocritical in any manner when applying the rehat to our own personal lives.

4) WEDDING CEREMONY / ANAND SANSKAR (fourth ceremony)

In the ancient past, society was divided into four caste groups and four stages of life (child, student, householder/family and spiritual/old age) for the effective functioning of all tasks. The life of a celibate holy man was considered the highest lifestyle and the accepted method to reach God. The householder's life was considered as the worst lifestyle and it was thought to be an obstacle on the path to spiritual enlightenment. It was this teaching that forced Kings like Partharee and Gopi Chand to give up their kingdoms, get their ears pierced and live in jungles. However, having done this and wandering with a stick in one hand and a satchel over their shoulder, begging for food, they still ended up crying in anguish:

"The King cries after getting his ears pierced.
He goes from house to house begging for sustenance."
(SGGSJ Ang 954)

By detaching yourself from ordinary life, leaving your home and surviving off wild fruits in jungles, the love of God is not achieved and even the love of sin is not removed in this way:

"Abandoning his household, he may go to the forest, and
live by picking fruit; But even so, his sinful evil mind
does not renounce sin."
(SGGSJ Ang 855)

"You call her mother, but are lured by the three senses,
the mind, the eyes and the ears. The mind wants sexual
contact with a woman, the eyes want to see an attractive

49

woman & the ears want to hear the sweet words of a woman." (SGGSJ Ang 903)

The person still remains entangled in sin. Many 'holy men' have gone and lived in jungles, yet they regretted doing so and Satguru says:

"Instead of wearing these beggars' robes,
it is better to be a householder, and give to others."
(SGGSJ Ang 587)

Going to live in the jungles would be of use if God Himself lived in the jungle. God is to be attained within yourself, by tuning into the Shabad, so what need is there to go anywhere else? This is why Bhagat Farid has said living in jungles is a waste of time:

"Fareed Jee says, why do you wander from jungle to jungle, crashing through the thorny trees? The Lord abides in the heart; why are you looking for Him in the jungle?" (SGGSJ Ang 1378)

"Why do you go looking for Him in the forest? Although He is unattached, He dwells everywhere. He is always with you as your companion. Like the fragrance which remains in the flower, and like the reflection in the mirror, the Lord dwells deep within; Search for Him within your own heart, O Siblings of Destiny."
(SGGSJ Ang 684)

The destruction of ego is to be achieved by immersing your heart in Naam then God is attained.

"Ego is opposed to the Name of the Lord;
The two cannot dwell in the same place."
(SGGSJ Ang 560)

A question was posed to Sri Guru Nanak Dev Jee, why doesn't Naam become imbued in our hearts? Guru Jee replied:

"You have a love for making gold jewellery, you have a love for making silver dishes, you have a love for lusting after the opposite sex and a love for putting sandalwood fragrance on." (SGGSJ Ang 15)

When all exterior tastes, desires and attachments have been extinguished, then God's Naam will become imbued in your heart and reveal itself. God will become self-revealed at this point. The aim is to stay detached from worldly passions and to imbue Naam into the mind, not to wonder uselessly in jungles. This is why Satguru Jee says

"A Sikh is to be a householder, if the Sikh is a true Sikh (i.e. a Brahmgyani) and one meets such a Sikh. One is to surrender at the feet of such a Sikh and do their seva in humility." (Bhai Gurdas Jee Var. 6, Pauri 2)

The Gurus stayed detached from worldly passions whilst living the life of householders and preached the same message to their Sikhs:

"Self-realisation is not obtained by wearing saffron robes; Nor is it obtained by wearing dirty robes. Guru Jee says, by following the teachings of the True Guru at home you achieve self-realisation."
(SGGSJ Ang 1421)

"Guru Jee says, meeting the True Guru, one comes to realise perfect knowledge.   While; laughing, playing, dressing and consuming fine foods, one is liberated."
(SGGSJ Ang 522)

Today many people have forgotten the above teachings and started to live outside the boundaries laid down by Gurmat, doing what they feel is right or wrong. Some Amritdharee Sikhs marry non-Amritdharees just for money but this is not acceptable, marriage should not be based upon desire for wealth or other worldy goods.   A marriage is to be based on the same Dharam/Principles and qualities in both people.

According to Gurmat both the bride and bridegroom should be Amritdharee.   The Kurmayee/Engagement should be a good deed and not involve taking money from your daughters/sisters. No form of dowry (gifts from the Brides family) should be given or accepted. Bhai Sahib Singh Jee writes in a Rehatnama:

"Sri Guru Gobind Singh Jee says, the Sikh that marry's his daughter to a Sikh, and does not take any money, He is a true Sikh of mine and will reach my abode in Sachkand." (Bhai Sahib Singh Rehatnama p.160)

The bride and bridegroom should be Amritdharee, follow the Rehat, recite Nitnem and as much additional Gurbani as possible and have knowledge of Sikh history. Besides their Rehat, their principles, age, education, appearance and other qualities are to be taken into consideration.

Ideally, the bride should be about four years younger than the bridegroom.[57] At the Kurmayee/engagement the bride's family are to give the bridegroom a token gift of five Rupees (£, $ etc) and a Kirpan with a gatra. The groom's family should give the bride a token gift of five Rupees (£, $ etc), a kangha and a kirpan with a Gatra.

At the time of the Kurmayee, the groom's family should have the Bhog of a Sehaj Paath or Akhand Paath at the Kurmayee. After the Bhog, Karah Parsaad must be distributed and Kirtan sung. However, if for any reason an Akand Paath or Sahej Paath cannot be performed, then the Kurmayee must be conducted in the presence of Sri Guru Granth Sahib Jee.

"Whatever needs doing, make a supplication in front of the Lord. 'May you make perfect what I am about to do', this is Satguru Jee's true teaching."
(SGGSJ Ang 91)

Similar shabads should be recited. Following a Hukamnama, the groom should be given the five rupees and kirpan with a gatra. The following shabad should be recited simultaneously:

"Oh my beloved Lord, please grace me with the presence of those saints, by the meeting of whom; my tongue may continuously recite Naam."
(SGGSJ Ang 743)

---

[57] This is a guide and not fixed. It is stated as generally females mature more quickly than men. Marrying partners of different ages is not frowned upon but as a generalisation for normal human relations this age guide has been provided.

Only Karah Parshad is to be distributed. Eating dates, putting on a Tilak (Hindu marking on the forehead), singing inappropriate songs, whistling, playing sinful music are all prohibited. On such happy occasions drinking alcohol, eating meat and other sinful activities are not to be undertaken. The giving and taking of clothes, jewellery etc is prohibited.

When the couple are ready to enter marriage, then the relations of both families are to meet and collectively decide on a date. They should not pay any notice to superstitions[58] and should stay within Gurmat.

"You calculate the auspicious days, but you do not understand that the One Creator Lord is above these auspicious days."
(SGGSJ Ang 904)

On the wedding invitation "God is One – He is realised by the True Guru's Grace" is to be written, by which all obstacles are removed and the event is successfully completed. According to the capabilities of the families, an Akhand Paath or Sehaj Paath should be held a few days before the Anand Karaj. During this happy occasion "Vadhans of the 4th Guru Ghoreean" is to be sung and other Gurbani of a similar nature is to be recited, at the bride and bridegrooms homes. Folk songs are not to be sung and only Gurbani is to be recited. The bride is not to wear any jewellery and make-up. Bindi and the wearing of sarees is not allowed. The bridegroom's family is to perform Ardas, take a Hukamnama from Sri Guru Granth Sahib Jee and then start their journey for the wedding. The marriage party of the bridegroom is to be small. Playing

---

[58] Looking for dates which are auspicious according to astrology and other such superstitions

54

dirty songs, hiring female dancers, doing bhangra and dancing are prohibited.

The following superstitions are not to be heeded to – making pigtails of grass, pouring oil, and wearing a Sehra (chaplet). Many argue that Sri Guru Gobind Singh Jee wore a Sehra around His head at His wedding and Gurdwara Sehra Sahib at Anandpur Sahib has been built to commemorate this. But this practice was prevalent before 'Khande dee Pahul'[59] was prepared, after which wearing a Sehra was prohibited.

Money is not to be waved over the heads of either the bride or bridegroom. The following superstitions/practices are also prohibited:

1. Wearing a Kalgi
(which was worn by Guru Gobind Singh Jee as a sign of his Sovereignty)[60];

2. Giving a ceremonial bath to the bride or bridegroom on the eve of the wedding and breaking objects after the bath;

3. Putting on a paste prepared with oil, barley flour and turmeric, popularly referred to as 'Maiya(n)';

4. Drinking water/milk after waving it over the heads of the bride/bridegroom; and

---

[59] Amrit prepared by Panj Pyare with a Khanda
[60] Only Guru Sahib is our sovereign and we thus do not wear a kalgi as we are His servants. On the day of the Anand Karaj some ill-advised Sikhs wear the Kalgi to the Gurdwara and only remove it after entering the Darbar Sahib (court of the Guru) – this is highly disrespectful to Sri Guru Granth Sahib Jee. Guru Sahib is our sovereign and we are to go to Guru Sahib in humility – thus the Kalgi should never be worn in the Gurdwara Sahib.

5. Bowing to the shrines of ancestors/saints etc.

These useless actions are not to be performed.

When the bridegroom and his family arrive at the place of the wedding ceremony, the following shabad is to be read,

"My friends have come into my home"
(SGGSJ Ang 764)

Other similar Shabads are also to be recited.

Upon arrival at the house of the bride, all are to greet each other by saying "Gurfateh" to one another. Money is not to be thrown. An Ardas is to be performed to ensure a smooth running ceremony proceeds, this is the Milni of Gursikhs. The singing of abusive songs ridiculing the bridegroom's family by the bride's family, or tying a ribbon to hold the bridegroom's family back from entering, are all prohibited. Food is to be eaten after reciting the following Salok,

"By coming under the sanctury of the Lord; Lust, anger, greed, emotional attachment and ego are eradicated. Upon the blessing of Sri Guru Ram Das Jee is the sanctuary of the Lord attained."(SGGSJ Ang 269)

After eating, water is to be offered to cleanse hands and mouths and Ardas is to be performed. The wedding is to be performed at the Gurdwara, regardless of the size of the house of the bride. If it is not possible to perform the Anand Karaj at a Gurdwara, only then is the house of the bride to be used for the wedding[61]. Sri Guru Granth Sahib

---

[61] Weddings in homes are prevalent in Punjab, India

Jee should be seated in the cleanest and nicest place in the home.

"Let yourselves be joined to the Name of the Lord;
Become Gurmukhs, spread out a mat (floor covering)
for Sadh Sangat to sit down and meditate."
(SGGSJ Ang 1185)

In line with Gurmat both families are to respectfully sit in the presence of Guru Sahib. The bride is to enter the Darbar Sahib with her face uncovered and bow to Sri Guru Granth Sahib Jee. The bridegroom and bride are to sit in front of Guru Sahib. The bridegroom is to sit on the right and the bride to his left. They should sit on the same level as the Sangat and not on any raised platform/spread. After both have been seated, the couple and their father's (uncles, brothers or cousins may stand in their place if required) are to stand for an Ardas for the commencement of the Anand Karaj.

4.1) The Recital of Paath, Parkarma and practical teachings

The Granthi recites the first verse of the Lava[62] and the couple are to listen to it whilst remaining seated. After completing the verse, the Granthi Singh is to place the Rumala back over Sri Guru Granth Sahib Jee. The Ragee Singh is to perform Kirtan of the first Lav and the couple are to slowly walk around Sri Guru Granth Sahib Jee (keeping Guru Sahib to their right-hand side), after which they are to bow to Guru Sahib and be seated. The bride is to walk by herself, around Guru Sahib, without any

---

[62] A four Verse Prayer, authored by the Fourth Guru, Sri Guru Ram Das Jee

assistance. Nobody is to stand whilst this is occurring. The bride is not to cover her face at any point.

The Granthi Singh is then to recite the second Lav and the Ragees are then to sing the second Lav in the same manner as the first. This is to be repeated for the third and fourth Lavs. After the recital of each Lav it is essential that the Granthi Singh replaces the Rumala back over Sri Guru Granth Sahib Jee.

If Ragee Singhs cannot be found, then the Granthi Singh is to recite each Lav, place the Rumala over Guru Sahib and then recite "Satnam, Vaheguru" whilst the couple walk/circumbabulate around Guru Sahib. The four Lavs are to be performed in this manner.

Whilst the couple are walking around Guru Sahib, the Granthi Singh is not to get up and leave the throne of Guru Sahib, upon which he is doing seva. Some unintelligent/superstitious people think by the Granthi Singh remaining seated on the throne of Guru Jee, he some-how also 'weds' the bride. The Granthi Singh is the Minister of Guru Sahib, the bride cannot become married to him as her hand was already asked for marriage by the bridegroom and also prior to the Lavs she held the 'Pula' (tassel) of the bridegroom so she is committed to marrying him.

The couple must walk around Sri Guru Granth Sahib Jee, many misguided people remain seated and perform the Anand Karaj in this way. This is against Gurmat and should never be done.

"Those feet that do Parkarma (circumambulations in a clockwise direction) of Guru Sahib Jee are priceless."
(Kabit Svaye Bhai Gurdas Jee p.17)

Walking around Satguru Jee (circumbabulating/Parkarma) signifies the sacrificing of ones mind, body and wealth. The circumambulating is a mark of respect signifying that Guru Sahib is greater than ourselves, as we have to take many steps to walk in humility around the throne of Sri Guru Granth Sahib Jee. The couple are begging for protection and assistance and signifying that they are the servants of Guru Sahib. If Parkarma is not performed during a time of happiness, then when will it ever be done? Parkarma are not to be performed around a fire, or any deity, persons, idols etc.

After the Lavs, whilst the Ragees are singing Shabads, the Granthi Singh is to mentally recite the 40 verses of Anand Sahib whilst sitting in the presence of Guru Sahib (upon Guru Jee's throne). If there are no Ragee Singhs then the Anand Sahib is to be recited out aloud to the sangat. Teachings are to be given to the couple (about how they should proceed in their lives as a married couple, which are in accordance with Gurmat). If a person is remarrying, the same ceremony is still to be performed including Lav's around Sri Guru Granth Sahib Jee. A list of relatives is not to be read out. An Ardas is to be performed and a Hukamnama read, then Karah Parshad is to be distributed afterwards.

On this happy occasion, the couple is to listen attentively to the Gurmat teachings given to them for successful guidance in both worldly and spiritual realms. Meritorious things that should be done by the couple are, practice of good actions, practising religion, taking good vows, performing meditation etc. Only good actions that will please Satguru are to be enacted – by the doing of which our lives will become blissful. Here is a more detailed account of what can be told to the couple:

1. Actions

*"One who calls himself a Sikh of the Guru, the True
Guru, should rise in the early morning hours
and meditate on the Lord's Name."*
(SGGSJ Ang 305)

The whole of the above Shabad is to be read out.

*"Only actions of religion are to be undertaken and those
actions which put us into confusion and condemnation
from God, are to be refrained from. Collect the goodness
by doing simran (meditation) at all times, then your mind
will deter from commiting sin."*
(Sri Dasam Granth Ang 710)

**"The Gurmukh is blessed with the Naam,
charity and purification."
(SGGSJ Ang 942)**

All your sins are washed away by meditating, and through
giving charitable donations, your hard work bears fruit.

*"One who works for what he eats & gives some of what
he has to charity, He/She realises the true path."*
(SGGSJ Ang 1245)

One tenth of your time and earnings should be given to the
preaching of Sikhi, Guru's Langar and all types of charity
connected to the Guru's House. In this way your virtuous

ambitions in life will be realised. On the other hand if nothing is given to charitable purposes then:

"Those who do not give money to the house of Sri Guru Nanak Dev Jee and/or charity, they will have their money taken by thieves or in fines to the government."
(Bachitar Natak, Sri Dasam Granth, Ang 71)

Not giving money for charitable purposes is on a par with being prosecuted, stealing, becoming diseased and success will not last. Therefore it is essential to donate, but it is to be given out of an honest living.

"Kabeer Jee says, those houses in which neither the Holy nor the Lord are served, are like cremation grounds; demons dwell within them."
(SGGSJ Ang 1374)

By having Ishnaan, the body is cleansed and laziness is removed. Ishaan is an integral action to Sikh life as we have to do Ishnaan in the morning before a prayer recital and many do Ishnaan before reciting any Paath (if they have been to the toilet so that their body is purified before reading[63] and touching Gurbani scriptures.) A Sikh is also to continually cleanse their self by eradicating sinful actions by remembering the teachings of the Guru and meditating on God at all times.

2. Religion

There are two types of religion. Firstly, common religious practice which is universal for all i.e. remembering God, earning an honest living and doing seva of mankind. Secondly, are individual religions such as that of Hinduism, Islam, Christianity etc. Gursikhs also have

---

[63] Thus one may do Ishnaan many times in a day and not just the one mandatory Ishnaan in the morning

their own religion – by taking Amrit from the Panj Pyare and keeping the discipline of the five Kakkaars, abstaining from the four cardinal sins, meditating on Naam and Gurbani and seeing only Sri Guru Granth Sahib Jee as their Guru. This is the religion of Gursikhs, which is more important to them than their lives, for example Bhai Mati Das Jee, Bhai Dyal Das Jee, Bhai Mani Singh Jee, Bhai Taru Singh Jee and many others have become martyrs but they did not compromise their faith.

3. Vows and regular practices

Some people go to places of pilgrimage and make vows for giving up something and make it a regular habit. One may say that from today I will not eat bananas, another may say that for the next six months I will not wear shoes etc. Gursikhs should make vows and regular practices, but of the following kind:

"Out of all the lights which is the best light - in the courtyard of the mind? The light of the knowledge of God is supreme. Meditation, meditation – which is the sublime meditation? Sublime is the meditation on the Name of the Lord, Har, Har. Renunciation, renunciation – which is noble renunciation? Noble is the renunciation of sexual desire, anger and greed. Begging, begging – what is noble begging? It is noble to beg for the action to praise the Lord, from the Guru. Awakening, awakening – which is the supreme awakening? The supreme awakening is to sing the Lord's praises. Attachment, attachment – which is the sublime attachment? Sublime is the attachment of the mind to the Guru's Feet. He alone is blessed with this way of life, upon whose forehead such destiny is recorded. Guru Jee says, everything is sublime and noble, for one who enters the Sanctuary of God."
(SGGSJ Ang 1018)

The Third Guru, Sri Guru Amar Das Jee uttered the following to a Pandit,

"On the ninth day of the month, make a vow to speak the Truth, and your sexual desire, anger and desire shall be vanquished."(SGGSJ Ang 1245)

The above is only the first line of the Shabad, Sri Guru Amar Das Jee went on to give further enlightenment to the Pandit to take on good actions on different days, to break superstitions associated with different days and to continuously develop spiritual and moral character. Speaking the truth and refraining from lying should be considered a vow. Gursikhs are to make a routine of reading as much Gurbani as possible, waking up in the ambrosial hours, doing Naam Simran, being charitable, performing Ishnaan of the body and soul, ridding themselves of vices and remain within the moral constraints laid down by Gurmat.

4. Fasts

Some fast according to movements of the moon, others on the birthdays of Krishan and Ram, others on the twelfth or fourteenth day of a lunar fortnight, some on a full moon, some on Sangrand and others on Tuesday's. Muslims fast over Ramadan. In Gurmat keeping any of these fasts is prohibited, and only the following 'fasts' are permitted:

"Sleeping little, eating little and speaking little is the way of enshrining Gurmat."
(Bhai Gurdas Jee, Var. 28, Pauri 15)

"Eating & sleeping little, helping the needy, forgiving others, being compassionate are all acts of a Sikh."
(Dasam Granth Ang 709)

63

"They break bonds of the world (thus gaining self-realisation) and achieve this by eating& drinking little."
(SGGSJ Ang 467)

(a) Male fast/abstinence: male youth are to make a habit of,

"Be faithful to your one wife, see others as your daughters and sisters, (for women be faithful to one husband and see others as your sons and brothers)."
(Var. 6, Pauri 8, Bhai Gurdas Jee)

*"Men should look at the opposite sex
as mothers, sisters and daughters,
(women should look at the opposite sex
as fathers, brothers and sons)."*
(Var. 29, Pauri 11, Bhai Gurdas Jee)

*"The wealth of another is like a stone to us, it is of no
use. Other women are like our mothers."*
(Dasam Granth, Ang 842)

"Do not gaze upon anothers wife, in a sinful way."
(SGGSJ Ang 274)

*"Like the companionship of a poisonous snake, so is the
desire for another's spouse, as the snake will poison/bite
you, causing harm, in the same way having sex with
another outside of marriage will cause much harm to
you."* (SGGSJ Ang 403)

These teachings are illustrated by the story of Bhai Sant
Ram Jee, a Sikh from the time of the fifth Guru, Sri Guru
Arjan Dev Jee:

"The tenth Guru, Sri Guru Gobind Singh Jee says that in the times of the fifth Guru, there was a Sikh called Sant Ram, whom worked as a bodyguard for the Emperor Jahangir. Jahangir's daughter became attracted to this Sikh and wanted to marry him, so Jahangir told the Sikh to convert to Islam, for the marriage to go ahead. The Sikh refused and was decapitated. Jahangir then took the Sikh's head on a platter to his daughter. His daughter edged forward to touch the face of the Sikh and his head floated a few inches away, thus not even accepting her in death." (Dasam Granth)

(b) Female fast/abstinence:

"Other than her husband, she knows no man.
She enshrines love for the True Guru,
and sees all others (men aswell) as the wives of God."
(SGGSJ Ang 54)

"There is one Husband Lord, and all are His brides[64]."
(SGGSJ Ang 933)

"Guru Jee says, she who looks upon Her Husband as the Lord, is blessed and has firm faith; great are those wives and they are received with honour in the Court of the Lord." (SGGSJ Ang 185)

Mai Sevan, Bibi Rajni, Mai Bhag Kaur and others stories illustrate this firm faith, of serving one's Husband as God[65].

---

[64] Thus you only have one Husband to whom you should be faithful, but similarily we only have One Lord whom we should all be faithful to - God.

[65] This needs to be taken in context, in a spiritual sense we are all brides of God and we are to renounce the world's attachments and go to our real home the abode of God (whilst alive we aim to achieve

At the time of holding the 'pula' the bride is promising to:

"Beloved husband if you take my hand;
I shall never forsake You. "
(SGGSJ Ang 322)

Husband – if you are holding my hand in marriage then I will not leave your side until the day I die.

The bridegroom promises to:

"Just like manmukhs leave the Lord and go to hell.
If I leave you I will go to hell too. "
(SGGSJ Ang 322)

In the same way that scoundrels forget the Lord and go to hells – in the same way if I leave your innocent side then I will suffer the pain of many hells.[66]

---

this). In the Indian context women usually leave their homes and go to the homes of their husbands family's, thus women should use this as an analogy of going to the abode of God and renouncing their previous attachments of their household and fully immerse themselves in serving their husband and seeing their husband as God. Obviously this can only work if the husband is religious, of high moral character and all decisions in the household should be based upon sound judgement in line with Gurmat, conversely the husband should treat his wife respectfully and act in accordance with Gurmat. This analogy can only work if both partners act out their respective roles correctly.

[66] This has all got to be taken in context. Thus if your Husband is an alcoholic and abusive then obviously he is not the image of God, but if He is a Gursikh and practising Sikhi then he should be served as God. There is room for compromise but all compromise and agreement is to be based upon Gurmat, only Gurmat practices are to be adhered to.

5. Meditation/Worship

*"Some worship idols and some worship the dead.
The world is entangled in false actions with no one
realising the true Lord."*
(Dasam Granth Ang 15)

In the Hindu religion, the worship of statues was started by
Narad Munee Jee.

*"The Hindus have forgotten the Primal Lord; they are
going the wrong way and have forsaken the true path.
They pray according to the teachings of Narad Jee,
performing idol worship."*(SGGSJ Ang 556)

Muslims also worship a stone in Mecca. In the same way if
people pray to deities and angels nothing is gained.

*"Why worship deities and angels,
O Siblings of Destiny?
What can we ask of them?
What can they give us?"*
(SGGSJ Ang 637)

Gursikhs have permission to:

*"Worship the One Divine Lord.
The true cleansing bath (which will eradicate our sins)
is service (seva) of the Guru."*
(SGGSJ Ang 484)

*"Perform worship & adoration by meditating on Naam;
Without Naam there is no worship and adoration."*
(SGGSJ Ang 489)

*"Worship the True Guru at all times & make Him happy.
By such service, I find peace in the Court of the Lord."*
(SGGSJ Ang 1158)

*"Pray to God - day and night do not think of any other,
enshrining pure love and faith. Fasting and praying to
tombstones/graves are not to be adhered to, even by
mistake."*

In Gurmat, the Timeless One is worshiped, discourse is of the Shabad (i.e. always thinking of or remembering Gurbani) and the vision is of the Khalsa. The bride and groom should have unbounded love and harmony so that they will achieve worldly and spiritual success. A union based simply on worldly concerns cannot be called a true union.

*"They are not said to be husband and wife,
who merely sit together."*
(SGGSJ Ang 788)

The couple can only be regarded as being in union if:

*"They alone are called husband and wife,
who have one light in two bodies."*
(SGGSJ Ang 788)

Compromise and decisions are to be made in the following manner:

*"Sikh husband and wife congregate
and discuss the boundless God.
Teaching their children how to meditate
by repeating His Name."*
(Rehatnama Bhai Sahib Singh Jee, p.160)

68

"The husband and wife are very much in love; sitting together, they make evil plans. All that is seen shall pass away. This is the Will of my God. How can anyone remain in this world forever? What can be done to prepare for the inevitable death? Serving the Perfect Guru, the body is purified. Guru Jee says, the Lord merges them into Himself; whom are absorbed in the Naam." (SGGSJ Ang 1250)

The couple should discuss their actions with one another before doing anything. The bride is to respect her in-laws as if they were her own parents and the bridegroom is to do the same with his in-laws, maintaining their love and a good relationship. All actions are to be discussed by the couple and they are to remain strictly in adherence with Gurmat. Then Satguru Jee will keep all their affairs on an upward spiral.

5) DEATH CEREMONY / ANTAM SANSKAR (fifth ceremony)

"Death comes to all, and all must suffer separation."
(SGGSJ Ang 595)

(Some of the comments below may not apply to those outside of Punjab/India. The translation is made according to the original text, thus take this into account when thinking of a funeral in other countries.)

If an Amritdharee is dying and has lived their life in accordance to the Rehat Maryada then their life has been worthwhile. But if a person is not Amritdharee or has committed a cardinal sin then they should re-take Amrit from the Panj Pyare. Gurbani is to be continually recited by the bedside of the dying person. If the person is entangled in worldly affairs and the false love of friends/relatives is affecting them then the second Astpadi of Sukhmani Sahib starting with:

*"Where there is no mother, father, children,
friends or siblings, for support ..."*
(SGGSJ Ang 264)

is to be recited.

This is to be recited continuously and if the person is highly spiritual (i.e. meditates and has knowledge of Gurmat) then the twenty first Astpadi is to be read:

"When this world had not yet appeared in any form ..."
(SGGSJ Ang 290)

After the death of the person, you should not cry, wail or beat your chests in bereavement. The person is not to be lowered from their bed, Guru Amar Das Jee said that;

"If one cries upon my death (passing), it will not be
pleasing to me, as they have not understood
the essence of life and death"
(SGGSJ Ang 923)

If you cry after the dead, the tears that you cry become an ocean in the after-life for the deceased, these tears blow out the light of the soul and the 'path' becomes shrouded in darkness. For this reason crying and wailing is prohibited. For the good of the deceased Gurbani Nitnem is to be recited – with which the departed will be assisted in the after-world. Gurbani kirtan is to be recited:

"When a Sikh dies, their body must be bathed.
Their Kacchera must be changed and turban tied.
While doing this Sri Japji Sahib
must be continuously recited."
(Rehatnama Bhai Deya Singh Jee, p.76)

Whilst washing the deceased's body, Japji Sahib is to be recited at all times. When the Kashera is changed, one leg is to be removed first and then the dry, fresh Kashera put on. The 5 Kakkar – Kirpan on gatra, Kashera, Kangha in hair, Kara on arm and a Kurta/Chola are to be put on, a turban around the head and a parna around the neck are to be put on the deceased. In addition to this a Kamarkasa/waistband is to be tied and a second fresh dry Kashera is to be tied around the waist with another cloth.[67] All clothes should be of good quality and well tailored.

---

[67] The second Kashera is tied as this is the way of a Khalsa who lives a life of being 'tyar bar tyar' or being prepared for every eventuality at all times. So Sikhs who live this lifestyle wear a spare kashera around

After performing Ardas the body is to be taken to the funeral pyre/crematorium. For the respect of Gurbani the head of the deceased is to be placed towards the Ragees and his/her feet in the opposite direction, the feet are not to be placed in the direction of those reading Gurbani. If Ragee Singhs cannot be booked then "Satnam – Vaheguru" is to be recited aloud along the way.

On the way to the pyre, the body is not to be put on the floor, a water pitcher is not to be broken, there is to be no crying/wailing, spilling of water, bowing down and the breaking of a piece of kitchen-wear etc are all prohibited. If there is a Gurdwara on the way, then the body can be placed on the floor outside the Gurdwara, so a final salutation to the Guru can be made.

The pyre is to be made of wood, which shouldn't have been used to move cow-dung; i.e. fresh wood is used. If possible sandalwood and ghee/pure butter are to be placed on the pyre. After placing the deceased on the pyre, one Singh is to recite Japji Sahib whilst facing the head of the deceased. The others are to prepare the pyre and listen to the prayer. When the pyre is ready and Japji Sahib completed, Ardas is to be performed:

"Oh True King bless this person, forgive all the sins that they have committed in their life. Bless the deceased with abode in your blessed feet, give strength to the family to accept your will, give us permission to set the pyre alight."

---

their waste in the manner described. Some may argue of what the point of doing this is upon the deceased. It is similar to dressing the individual with all their other clothes and in the attire of the Khalsa – those clothes will also perish in the funeral pyre when cremated.

The pyre is then lit. Screaming and wailing is not allowed and matches are not to be set alight and needlessly thrown. Satnam Vaheguru or Kirtan is to be continuously recited. When the pyre is half burnt Kirtan Sohela is to be recited and Ardas performed. The skull of the burning body is not to be cracked open.

Upon returning from the cremation, all should go straight to the Gurdwara and have Ishnaan. If this is not possible, then the hands, feet and face should be washed.

Karah Parshad is to be prepared and brought into the presence of Sri Guru Granth Sahib Jee, after which Shabads about death are to be recited. Ardas is to be performed and Karah Parshad distributed. Reciting Gurbani on behalf of the deceased is essential. If possible, a Sehaj Paath is to be started on the day of the cremation[68]. If one has the capability of organising an Akhand Paath, then it is to be started on the eighth day after the cremation and the Bhog on the tenth day, after which Ramkali Sadh is recited, Ardas performed and Karah Parshad distributed. During the making or preparation of the Karah Parshad, all forty verses of the Anand Sahib are to be recited (as is normal).

Superstitions about doing something on the twelfth, thirteenth or seventeenth day after the cremation are not to be performed. The Khalsa is supreme, therefore doing something on the tenth day is in accordance with the Guru's command.

---

[68] In the Western world cremations may take place many days after the person has died, thus a Sehaj Paath/Akhand Paath Bhog may not take place 10 days after the death of the person. The cremation must take place before the Bhog of the Paath.

Women are not to cry and wail. They should accept God's will. All the family of the deceased should sit and listen to the Paath. The family is to serve the Granthis to the best of their abilities. At the time of the Bhog, good clothing and money is to be presented as an offering infront of Guru Sahib Jee.

After the second day, Jaitsari di Var (two Saloks daily) and Sahskriti (six Saloks daily) should be recited and the meanings explained each morning. If there is no one available to make these discourses, then the whole of 'Jaitsari di Var' and 'Sahskriti' is to be read on the day of the person's death. If the person died somewhere else, all of 'Jaitsari di Var,' 'Vadhans di Var' and 'Sahskriti Salok's' are to be recited after collecting up the ashes. The tenth Guru, the Father of the Khalsa, made this a rite of the Khalsa, enshrining it into the Rehat.

The ashes are to be collected as they are and are not to be foiled with. The tying of strings, placing nails in soil etc are prohibited (superstitions). Kirpan and Kara are not to be picked out of the ashes, the ashes are to be collected as they are. All the ashes (and bones) are to be collected and taken to either Kiratpur Sahib or Goindval Sahib and scattered in the river. If this is not possible, then they can be scattered in any nearby flowing river/stream. The ashes are not to be placed in the Ganges[69] and a shrine/memorial stone is not to be made.

---

[69] In hope of salvation some place their ashes in the Ganges as is tradition amongst other faiths in India. For Sikhs the popular places for ashes dispersal are Kiratpur Sahib and Goindval Sahib, but we can disperse our ashes anywhere in the world in flowing water. So the reference to the Ganges is to make clear that it holds no special significance for the Sikhs to disperse their ashes there.

6) RESPECTING GURBANI (summarised)

"The Word, the Bani is Guru, and Guru is the Bani. Within the Bani all the Ambrosial Nectar is contained. If His humble servant believes, and acts according to the Words of the Guru's Bani, then the Guru, in person, emancipates him." (SGGSJ Ang 982)

> *"That person who does not respect and fear Gurbani is not a Sikh."*
> (Gurpartap Suraj Granth)

At Sri Anandpur Sahib, a Singh was reading Gurbani slightly wrong and Sri Guru Gobind Singh Sahib Jee said, "Oh Singh! You are breaking my limbs." This is why Guru Sahib Jee taught and explained all the meanings and correct discourses of Gurbani to a number of Singhs. The chosen Singh's would then pass on this knowledge, understanding and correct pronunciation of Gurbani to all.

"Oh Sikhs, listen to this teaching - recite Gurbani correctly (i.e. pronounce it correctly). Read it and obtain many pleasures, herein and thereafter."

Satguru Jee gave the utmost respect to Gurbani in all his ten forms. In the same way, we should also strive to show the same respect. In order to do this, the following should be adhered to:

- No one should seat themselves upon Guru Jee's throne without having bathed or washing their feet. Nor should they do so whilst wearing socks or gloves.

- A person who has had sex or a nightly emission should have a full Ishnaan (from head to toe, including washing hair), wash their clothes, then recite Japji Sahib and then do an Ardas. Then they are ready to go and sit behind Guru Jee's throne.

- Some ignorant people, under the influence of bad company they keep, masturbate. This leads to problems with ejaculation and is a sin, therefore masturbation should never be performed.

- If your hands have touched your, or someone else's, feet, face, Kashera or if they are wet or dirty, then they must not to be placed on Sri Guru Granth Sahib Jee, Pothis (volumes of Granths) or Gutka sahibs (collections of bani's).

- Whilst in Guru Jee's Hazoori[70] nothing is to be eaten or placed in the mouth, i.e. sweets or cardamom.

- A Sikh sitting in Guru Jee's Hazoori is not to sit on any form of cushion. He/she is not to put his feet under the Manji Sahib (Guru's Sahib's platform/throne) or lean against it in any way. He/she is to sit cross-legged without leaning on anything.

- You must never put your feet in the direction of Sri Guru Granth Sahib Jee.

Maharaj is never to be placed in a closet or cupboard, on the contrary, Guru Sahib must be placed on a nicely decorated throne in a well-ventilated room. Clothing appropriate to the season is to be placed upon the throne of Guru Jee. In the summer, thin clothing and in winter, warm clothing i.e. a thick blanket/duvet must be used.[71] If

_____

[70] Upon the Throne of Sri Guru Granth Sahib, in Guru Jee's presence/seva

[71] Some ill-advised Sikhs feel changing clothing/blankets according to the season is not necessary, but in our daily recital of Ardas – we proclaim to believe in Sri Guru Granth Sahib Jee as the living

Maharaj is kept in a palki then a small canopy is to be hung inside the palki and a larger one over the top of the palki. The canopy is placed as a mark of respect for Satguru Jee who is the Master of all beings. The spread that is placed under the palki and Manji Sahib[72] is to be of better quality, and separate, to that of the Granthi Singh. The Manji Sahib is to be well built and attractive in appearance.

Whenever Satguru Jee is brought somewhere, the Sangat are to remove their shoes and perform Kirtan. When Satguru Jee passes you are to rise and clasp you hands together as a mark of respect and are to humbly bow. For as long as you can see Satguru Jee, you are to remain standing with both hands clasped.

Whilst Satguru Jee is on the move, five Singhs are to accompany him at all times and they are to remain bare-footed. One Singh is to do Chaur Sahib Seva whilst one is to go ahead of Satguru Jee and sprinkle water. In order to make the Sangat aware that Satguru Jee is coming in their direction, gongs or other appropriate instruments are to be played.

When doing Paath from a Pothi or Gutka you should sit on a clean cloth placed on the floor. If there is a settee/bed or other furniture on a higher platform that you can sit on, then you should sit upon this furniture to recite Paath. Whilst sitting on the bed of another, Gurbani is not to be recited sitting directly behind them (i.e. with their back to you). You are not to recite Gurbani sitting on the floor when someone is sitting on a higher platform than yourself (at home) or facing the side of the bed where your feet are placed at night. When reciting Gurbani, you are to

---

embodiment of the 10 Gurus and it is with this in mind that all due respect to Guru Sahib is enacted.
[72] This is bed-like stand upon which Guru Jee is placed directly upon

face your pillow or the place where your head rests for sleep.

A person who gives Santhia (teaches how to correctly pronounce Gurbani) should not sit on a pillow or on a higher platform than those being taught. Pothi's of Gurbani, Gutka Sahibs, Sri Dasam Granth Gurbani, Bhai Gurdas Jee's writings are all to be given the utmost respect and care, this includes any other writings about Gurmat or those which contain Gurbani. Normal books are not to be stored along with scriptures of Gurbani. A Gutka is not to be used whilst having your head uncovered and/or with your shoes on. A bookmark or any form of sign is not to be kept in Sri Guru Granth Sahib Jee. Gutkas and Pothis of Gurbani are to be stored in a nice place, high up, towards which your feet will not be facing and where your back will not be turned against. Rumala's with images/pictures on them are not to be placed upon Sri Guru Granth Sahib Jee. Expensive, beautiful and clean Rumalas are to be offered to Guru Sahib. In the presence of Guru Sahib a candle of paraffin/white spirit is not to be lit.

When listening to Gurbani from a radio, cassette player (or CD/video etc) the audio-visual aid is to be placed on a higher platform than the person listening to it, as a mark of respect to the Gurbani being listened to. Newspapers, magazines, books etc in which Gurbani may be written are not to be thrown away or allowed to fly around on the ground – after use, they should be burnt and the ashes scattered in a flowing stream, river or ocean.

When going to sit in the Hazoori of Guru Sahib, clothing that was worn when going to the toilet is not to be worn (until washed again). After going to the toilet, the hands are to be washed 5 times with an appropriate aid (soap, sand). Dishes are to be cleaned with sand or soil and are not to only be cleaned with washing up powder (as used in India)[73]. Brushing your teeth daily is essential. After passing urine, it is essential to wash your hands.

Weapons are to be shown utmost respect. They are not to be kept in a place towards which your feet will face.

"Praying day and night thinking of no other (than the One Lord), enshrine pure love and faith. Fasting and praying to tombstones/graves are not to be adhered to even by mistake. Being charitable at places of pilgrimage, being compassionate, entering rituals of throwing things into a fire and being very superstitious about what one eats, are all of no avail if one is not recognising the One Lord. A Khalsa is one, whom has the love and light of God in one's heart, others are impure." (Dasam Ang 212)

Parshad from a tomb of a saint, grave or serpent, god/demi-gods is not to be eaten.

"He/She that eats Parshad from such a place
is not a Sikh."

In the same way no one is to be bowed to or believed in as your Guru other than Sri Guru Granth Sahib Jee. No belief is to be placed in your ancestors. In your homes, dirty photos/posters are not to be put up, rather photos of warriors, saints and the Satgurus are to be put up but your feet are not to be put in their direction. In Gurdwaras or at home, no photo is to be placed in front of Sri Guru Granth Sahib Jee. For an Amritdharee Sikh it is essential that he addresses another Amritdharee Sikh using their full name.

---

[73] This is relevant when washing steel or Sarab Loh utensils, as these cannot be effectively cleaned unless sand/soil is used.

A person who calls another by half their name or a nickname is punishable (full names should be printed on wedding cards):

"When a Sikh meets another Sikh,
they are to welcome one another by saying,
Vaheguru Jee Ka Khalsa, Vaheguru Jee Ki Fateh!"

A floor covering of animal dung, clay and hay (as is common in India) is never to be used where Sri Guru Granth Sahib Jee is to reside. Nor should they be placed in a room where the floor coverings have been made of these sorts of materials. Amritdharee women are not to go to 'Theean' – a ladies festival which is held on each Sunday of the Bikrami month of Savan and they are not to clap/dance, do Gidda etc (performing seva on a monthly basis is merely superstition and not due to respect of the Guru). Women should not sit in the Guru's Hazoori or do Chaur Sahib when they are menstruating.[74]

The Khalsa should keep away from people who sit on cushions or high platforms, or get people to bow to them in the presence of Sri Guru Granth Sahib Jee, or exorcise ghosts.

Khalsa Jee! Out of ones honest earned livings, giving one tenth in charity is essential, as is giving a tenth of our time to the service of Guru Sahib. Out of every twenty four hours, two and a half hours should be spent on meditation, performing and/or listening to Gurbani. The names of the ten Guru Sahibs, Panj Pyare, four Sahibzade

---

[74] They can continue to do all other tasks of normal life and attend the Gurdwara. It is only doing direct seva of Guru Sahib that is off the limits during this time. This is only done for purity reasons and keeping the uptmost respect for Guru Sahib – similarly men who are injured or ill would not also be allowed to conduct this seva too.

(princes of Sri Guru Gobind Singh Jee) and five Takhats are to be memorised.

6.1) Summary of the Rehat of Sri Guru Granth Sahib Jee, Akhand Paath & Sehaj Paath

To take Sri Guru Granth Sahib Jee from one place to another there are to be a minimum of 5 Singhs present with Guru Jee. A gong or other relevant instruments are to be played to make others aware of Guru Jee's arrival. Water is to be sprinkled in front of Guru Sahib. If you are taking Guru Sahib in a car/vehicle, then the container of water is to be placed in the car.

Where Sri Guru Granth Sahib Jee is present and Karah Parshad is to be prepared, the floor covering must not be made of inappropriate materials (e.g. in India, animal dung mixed with clay and hay is sometimes spread on a dirt floor to stop dust from flying around).

Once a suitable room is selected, the floor, walls and ceilings should be broomed, cleaned or washed appropriately. Where Sri Guru Granth Sahib Jee is Parkash[75], a beautiful canopy is to be placed over Guru Jee. If Guru Jee is Parkash in a Palki, then there should be a small canopy in the Palki and in turn a larger one is to be hung over the Palki.

Sehaj Paath
At the start/Arambh and end/Bhog of Sehaj Paath, Karah Parshad made of clarified (unsalted) butter/ghee is to be made. At the start of the Paath, the Ardas and Hukamnama must be recited followed by a minimum of

---

[75] Parkash = Present

five verses of Sri Japji Sahib, before distributing Karah Parshad. Upon completion of the Sehaj Paath, fives verses of Sri Japji Sahib and the last Salok (of Japji Sahib) are to be recited after the Raag Mala, and then the Ardas is performed.

When the person performing Ardas says,

"Food has been prepared with purity,
please do Bhog to the food and bless it Lord."
(SGGSJ Ang 1266)

Upon hearing this verse, the blade of the Kirpan is simultaneously 'placed' into the Parshad and out. In this manner the Karah Parshad is blessed by the Kirpan, a weapon which is also accepted as a form of the Guru. When placing the offered Rumalas over Sri Guru Granth Sahib Jee, the following is not to be recited,

"Oh Lord, you have given me this gift of love (silk cloth)
to cover my faults and keep my status."
(SGGSJ Ang 520)

This Shabad can only to be recited when a Siropa[76] is given to a person.

Sri Akhand Paath

An Akhand Paath is to be started by performing an Ardas and reciting a Hukamnama. After this the Granthi Singh is to immediately begin the Paath, there must not be

---

[76] This is the highest award given in Sikhi to somebody for some special fete of meditation or seva. It is usually a turban, the length of which signifies the Guru blessing you from head to toe and covering your faults.

any interruptions, breaks or request for permission from the Sangat nor should the Granthi utter the Fateh. The Karah Parshad is to be distributed only after the completion of Sri Japji Sahib.

At the start of "Jaitsari Dee Var" is Madh Bhog (halfway point of Sri Akhand Paath). Ardas is to be performed at this point as well, to mark the passing of half of the Akhand Paath, but the Paath remains continuous. Once the Raagmala and complete Japji Sahib have been recited at the Bhog (completion) of Sri Akhand Paath, a Jakara is not to be sounded and nor is the Fateh to be said.[77] The Ardas is to begin immediately. Fateh is only to be announced after the Hukamnama has been read. Shabad Kirtan or discourses on Gurmat are to be conducted. If Shabads of Arti are recited then candles/lamps are not to be lit and waved around.

Along side the Sri Akhand Paath, Sri Jap Jee Sahib must be continuously recited. Over the container of water, a coconut wrapped in white or saffron (not red) cloth is to be placed. Red string is not to be tied around the coconut or container. In order to create a pleasant atmosphere, incense sticks (air-fresheners, fragrances etc) should be used. At night time, there should be additional lighting provisions in case the light bulbs or electricity fails. Ghee lamps can be used, but those which use paraffin, white spirit or gas, should not be used in the same room as Sri Guru Granth Sahib Jee. None of the Paathis are to be non-Amritdharee

---

[77] The full Anand Sahib is to be silently recited near the Karah Parshad and should be read before the commencement of the Saloks of Sri Guru Tegh Bahadur Jee (Bhog de Salok) on Ang 1426. In the west it is now common practice for the full Anand Sahib to be read after the recital of Japji Sahib at many Gurdwaras. In both instances the Anand Sahib is read for the bhog to the Karah Parshad.

or those that have committed any of the cardinal sins (without having re-taken Amrit).

The Paathi Singhs are to wear clean clothing and must bathe before starting on their Paath seva. The Akhand Paath should be completed in approximately 48 hours[78]. The Granthi Singh is to be Amritdharee, passionate about Sikhi, perform Nitnem, meditation and have high levels of Gurmat knowledge.

Any financial and other offerings to the Paathis, should be of a reasonable level, enough to provide a respectable living. If the family listen to the Paath with 'love' and carry out seva themselves, and the Paathi Singhs are passionate and pronounce the Paath correctly, then the rewards are endless:

"Reading and listening to Gurbani
has the reward of many ages."
(SGGSJ Ang 546)

"Listening to Gurbani has the same merit
as thousands of good actions."
(SGGSJ Ang 238)

6.2) Raagmala

The spiritual light of the 10 Guru Sahibs is enshrined within Sri Guru Granth Sahib Jee and thus the commandments of Gurbani are to be adhered to. Gurbani is to be accepted as the Guru.

---

[78] This method of completing Akhand Paths within 48 hours has been in place since Sri Guru Tegh Bahadur Sahib Jee conducted an Akhand Path at Prayag (today known as Allahabad) for the birth of Sri Guru Gobind Singh Jee. It ensures that the Paathis are fluent and well versed in reading Gurbani.

Raagmala was authored by Guru Jee, first Sri Guru
Arjan Dev Jee Maharaj got Bhai Gurdas Jee to write an
edition of Aad Sri Guru Granth Sahib Jee – in which
Raagmala is present, it is written in the same ink, on the
same quality paper and in the same handwriting as the rest
of the Gurbani, this edition is now at Sri Kartarpur Sahib
(Doaba). Bhai Bano Jee copied that edition, which also
includes Raagmala. Sri Guru Gobind Singh Jee Maharaj at
Takhat Damdama Sahib got Bhai Mani Singh Jee to scribe
Sri Guru Granth Sahib Jee. On this occasion, Guru Jee
dictated the whole of the Sri Guru Granth Sahib Jee in
which Raagmala is present; it is also present in the 4
editions written by Shaheed Baba Deep Singh Jee. Those
that argue the poet Jodh wrote Raagmala in 'Madavanal
Kamkandla' or that the poet Alam wrote it, in actual fact
are mistaken. The poet Jodh wrote 'Madavanal
Kamkandla' in Sanskrit in the Hijra year 991 (Muslim
calendar), which is 1640 Bikrami in which Raagmala is not
present. The poet Aalam was one of Satguru Sri Guru
Gobind Singh Jee's 52 poets, he lived from 1712 Bikrami
to 1774 Bikrami. He wrote the Raagmala according to
what he heard spoken in the court of Sri Guru Gobind
Singh Jee. The poet Aalam lived 113 years after the first
edition of Sri Guru Granth Sahib Jee was compiled – how
do some argue that he wrote Raagmala 113 years before
the first edition? From this it is clear that Guru Sahib
wrote Raagmala. Bhai Sahib Bhai Vir Singh Jee in Sri Gur
Partap Suraj Granth from 2128 Ang to 2133 Ang in detail
explains why Raagmala was authored by Guru Jee. If one
were to read Giani Sahib Singh's (Dhamdan Sahib)
detailed discourse about the authenticity of Raagmala no
confusion and doubt would be left and one would surely be
convinced that Raagmala was written by Guru Jee and that
it is Gurbani. There is also a small book called "Raagmala
Gurbani Hai", published by Damdami Taksal, which

85

details the spiritual meaning of Raagmala and has arguments for any point that has ever been raised against Raagmala's authenticity.[79] For these reasons each and every Gursikh should accept Raagmala as Gurbani without any doubts.

FINAL NOTE: Sahib Sri Guru Gobind Singh Jee – our Tenth Father at Takhat Sri Damdama Sahib (Guru Ki Kanshi) from 1762 Katak Sudhi Puranmashi 'til 1763 Bikrami 23 Savan, for 9 months and 9 days dictated the whole of Sri Guru Granth Sahib Jee to Bhai Mani Singh Jee from memory. Baba Deep Singh Jee and Bhai Mani Singh Jee along with another 48 Singhs were taught by Guru Jee the correct meaning and pronunciations of Gurbani and blessed them with the wisdom of God (Brahm Gyan).

Guru Sahib then went to Sri Hazoor Sahib and blessed Sri Guru Granth Sahib Jee with the Gurgaddi, enthroning them as the Guru. Bhai Mani Singh Jee was sent to Amritsar, upon getting there he started the Taksal (seminary) of teaching the correct meanings and pronunciations of Gurbani. Baba Deep Singh did the same but was based at Takhat Sri Damdama Sahib. Both these Taksals have been operating under the leadership of Brahm Gyanis (Blessed souls with the knowledge of God). For these reasons the Code of Conduct narrated in this booklet is to be maintained and the commands of Sri Guru Gobind Singh Jee are to be accepted to make our lives worthwhile.

A more detailed version of the Code of Conduct can be found in "Gurbani Paath Darpan" and "Khalsa Jeevan".

---

[79] An English translation of the spiritual meanings of Ragmala has been detailed in a book by Kamalpreet Singh Pardeshi, 'Ragmala A Spiritual Composition.' (Publishers, dtfbooks.com)

7.0 Respecting Gurbani

The Guru's Word
(Full Version)

Foreword

It is with the grace of Sri Guru Granth Sahib Jee Maharaj that the translation of *'Gurbani Da Adab'* ('Respecting Gurbani') took place. The inspiration for this translation came from the 300th anniversary of Sri Guru Granth Sahib Jee's Gurta-Gurgaddi Divas in October 2008. Sri Guru Ram Das Jee writes:

The Word/Bani is the Guru and the Guru is the Bani.
Within the Bani all the Ambrosial Nectar is contained.
If a humble servant believes and acts according to the
Words of the Guru's Bani,
then the Guru, in person, emancipates that person."
(Sri Guru Granth Sahib Jee, Ang 982)

We as Sikhs are expected to believe, follow and accept the above declaration. However, the respect and honour that has been shown to Gurbani has rapidly deteriorated since 1708 AD, when Sri Guru Gobind Singh Jee Maharaj graced us with our Everlasting Satguru, *Sri Guru Granth Sahib Jee Maharaj*. Unfortunately, and quite tragically, this disrespect and ignorance is down to us - the self-proclaimed followers of the True Guru.

As we look back into Sikh history, we discover that the level of respect that was previously shown to Gurbani was supreme. Some misguided people may believe Gurbani to be mere words, however, Gurbani has always been revered in the most supreme manner, continually placed on palanquins and fanned with Chaur Sahib (whisk waved over Sri Guru Granth Sahib Jee, it is waved over Guru Jee out of respect, in the past such a whisk was waved over the heads of Kings- it is a sign of royalty and respect in the Indian sub-continent and other parts of the world). In this day and age, as the Sikh Panth is on a numerical rise, we find the same divine Gurbani being thrown away, vandalised on wedding cards, exploited in newspapers and, even worse, our Beloved Satguru – The King of Kings, is being placed in suitcases and taken to pubs and clubs, which support anti-Gurmat weddings. More recently, incidents of sacrilegious acts against Sri Guru Granth Sahib Jee in India have been occurring far too often, including acts of deliberate arson & pre-meditated disrespect of Guru Sahib.

The need for this publication is paramount, in order for us as individuals and as a nation to implement the supreme standards of respect that our Gurus instilled. We need to unite and realise that our only salvation in this world is Gurbani and we must ensure respect of Gurbani is implemented by ourselves and others. Without this realisation, we cannot increase the level of respect for Gurbani; without respect for Gurbani, we cannot be called disciples of Sri Guru Nanak Dev Jee.

Sri Guru Granth Sahib Jee, the Eternal Light of the world, continues to provide guidance for the whole of mankind. It is now our duty to endeavour to uphold respect, love and a firm belief in Gurbani and spread this throughout the world through the propagation of the teachings of Gurbani.

Acknowledgments

First and foremost: Sri Guru Granth Sahib Jee has been our guide & inspiration in translating this publication. Our heartfelt gratitude and thanks goes to Guru Sahib for being a source of inspiration and the Beacon of Light for us. May Guru Sahib continue to grace us with such seva and forever keep us in their immortal Charan (feet).

Although the following Gurmukh Singhs of Damdami Taksal would prefer to go unmentioned, it is our duty to include them and thank them for blessing us with this seva as it was the following Gurmukhs who gave us the agiyaa (permission) to start the translation of Gurbani Da Adab. We shall be forever grateful to Bhai Sahib Bhai Gurdial Singh Jee 'Madho Jee', Jathedar Bhai Sahib Bhai Nirvair Singh Jee, Bhai Sahib Bhai Pargat Singh Jee, Baba Gurdev Singh Jee 'Bapoo Jee' and Gyani Pritam Singh Jee 'Likhari'.

Throughout the translating and editing of this publication, there have been many times when we were unable to grasp the complete meaning and understanding of the Gurmukhi. On many occasions, we had to consult learned Gursikhs such as Bhai Sahib Bhai Balbir Singh Jee, Kathakaar Damdami Taksal, and other countless gupt Gursikhs ('gupt' means anonymous or those who want to remain so), who gave up their time to help us through the translating and editing of this publication. We pray, with our hands folded, that Satguru Sri Guru Granth Sahib Jee Maharaj blesses and keeps all those, who gave agiyaa and assisted us in the translation of this panthik booklet, in Chardikala (ascending high spirtis). May the Light of Satguru Jee reside within them forever.

It gives us great pleasure to dedicate this publication to the immortal memory of the supremely respected Saint, Baba Thakur Singh Jee Khalsa, acting leader of Damdami Taksal, whose lifetime of seva, simran, and Gursikhi Jeevan (discipline of this Sikh) will forever bear an everlasting impression on the Sikh nation.

Sukha Singh & Jaskeerth Singh

Respecting Gurbani

Bani emanated from the Primal Lord.
It eradicates all anxiety.
(Sri Guru Granth Sahib Jee Ang 628)

When Sri Guru Nanak Dev Jee uttered Bani,
light spread and the darkness was dispelled.
(Bhai Gurdas Jee, Vaar 1, Pauri 38?)

The True Guru respected the divine Bani in all Their Ten Forms – the following are examples of how each Guru respected Gurbani:

1. Sri Guru Nanak Dev Jee

During the time of the Goshts (discussions of Sri Guru Nanak Dev Jee with the Sidhs), the Sidhs asked Satguru Nanak Dev Jee;

Who is your Guru? Whose disciple are you?
(Sri Guru Granth Sahib Jee Ang 942)

The respected King (Guru Nanak Dev Jee) answered:

The Shabad is the Guru, upon whose vibration
I lovingly focus my consciousness as the disciple.
(Sri Guru Granth Sahib Jee Ang 943)

I have no support except of the Guru,
holy congregation, and Bani.
(Bhai Gurdas Jee, Vaar 1, Pauri 42)

Oh Sidhs! Without the Guru's congregation and without the Guru's Bani, there is no other support at all for us.

2. Sri Guru Angad Dev Jee

The Bhatts recited the following about the Second King, Sri Guru Angad Dev Jee:

> *Guru Nanak realised the Immaculate Naam,*
> *the Name of the Lord.*
> *He was lovingly attuned to loving devotional*
> *worship of the Lord.*
> *Guru Angad was with Him, life and limb, like the ocean;*
> *He showered His consciousness with*
> *the Word of the Shabad.*
> (Sri Guru Granth Sahib Jee, Ang 1406)

3. Sri Guru Amar Das Jee

Sri Guru Amar Das Jee says the following in 'Anand Sahib', from the daily Nitnem:

> *Come, O beloved Sikhs of the True Guru,*
> *and sing the True Word of His Bani.*
> *Sing the Guru's Bani, the supreme Word of all Words.*
> *Those who are blessed by the Lord's Glance of Grace -*
> *their hearts are imbued with this Bani.*
> (Sri Guru Granth Sahib Jee, Ang 920)

> *Gurbani is the Light to illuminate this world;*
> *by His Grace, it comes to abide within the mind.*
> (Sri Guru Granth Sahib Jee, Ang 67)

Sri Guru Amar Das Jee told Their Sahibzada (son), Baba Mohan Jee, to look after the Gurbani, which had been compiled by Sri Guru Amar Das Jee and by the previous two Guru Sahib Jees, as well as to make sure to not give this Gurbani to anyone apart from the Fifth Divine King, Sri Guru Arjan Dev Jee. Sri Guru Amar Das Jee blessed Sri Guru Arjan Dev Jee in Their childhood by saying:

My Grandson is the Boat of Gurbani.

Gurbani has been called the boat, which can liberate us from worldly beings:

The Guru is the Boat, and the Guru is the Boatman.
Without the Guru, no one can cross over.
(Sri Guru Granth Sahib Jee, Ang 1401)

4. Sri Guru Ram Das Jee

Sri Guru Ram Das Jee states:

The Word, the Bani is Guru, and Guru is the Bani.
Within the Bani, the Ambrosial Nectar is contained.
(Sri Guru Granth Sahib Jee, Ang 982)

The True Guru is the Word, and the Word is the True
Guru, teaching the Path of Liberation.
(Sri Guru Granth Sahib Jee, Ang 1309)

5. Sri Guru Arjan Dev Jee

The Fifth King, Sri Guru Arjan Dev Jee, personally went to Sri Goindwal Sahib to collect Pothia (Collections of Gurbani written by the previous Guru Sahibs) from Baba Mohan Jee. After receiving the Pothia, Guru Jee respectfully seated the Pothia on a palanquin. Guru Sahib Jee did not seat themselves on the same level as the Pothia, nor did Guru Jee ride Their horse back towards Amritsar Sahib. Instead, Guru Sahib Jee walked barefoot, keeping the palanquin to Their right, and waved a Chaur Sahib over the Pothia, until They arrived in Sri Amritsar Sahib. Guru Sahib Jee seated the ambrosial Gurbani on a platform at the place of Ath-Sath-Ghaat (a place within Sri Harimandar Sahib known as the place of 68 pilgrimages). Kirtan (hymn singing) was recited and the Gurbani Pothia were respected by reciting the following divine words:

These Pothia are the home
of the Transcendent Lord God.

(Sri Guru Granth Sahib Jee, Ang 1226)

After compiling and completing Sri Guru Granth Sahib Jee, the first Parkash of Sri Guru Granth Sahib Jee was performed at Sri Harimandar Sahib (NOTE: this is the first time Sri Guru Granth Sahib Jee was placed upon a throne to bless the congregation). Once this had taken place, Sri Guru Arjan Dev Jee never sat on a pillow in the presence of Sri Guru Granth Sahib Jee, or on the same level as Sri Guru Granth Sahib Jee. Guru Sahib Jee insisted that the Chaur Sahib was not waved over Them, but instead over Sri Guru Granth Sahib Jee, and then sat amongst the holy congregation. By showing great respect and reverence to Gurbani, the respected Fifth King blessed us with guidance on how to respect and revere Gurbani.

Near Sri Akaal Takhat Sahib is Kothri Sahib; here at night, on a daily basis, Sri Guru Granth Sahib Jee resumes the posture of bliss (Sukhaasan – takes rest after the day's ceremonies). Satguru Jee (Sri Guru Arjan Dev Jee) would not take rest on a bed alongside Sri Guru Granth Sahib Jee, but would instead lay a white sheet on the floor and rest below Sri Guru Granth Sahib Jee. To this day, a white sheet is kept on the floor alongside the bed of Sri Guru Granth Sahib Jee as a reminder of Their devotion.

The True King, Sri Guru Arjan Dev Jee, highlighted the greatness and supreme importance of Gurbani and gave this teaching to the Sikhs:

You cannot have Darshan (blessed sight) of the physical body of the respected Guru in all places or at all times. Know that Sri Guru Granth Sahib Jee is the Heart of the Guru, and is supreme, because Sri Guru Granth Sahib Jee will remain for all time. Know that Sri Guru Granth Sahib Jee's form is greater than mine; know and respect Sri Guru Granth Sahib Jee as the embodiment of the Lord.

Worship Sri Guru Granth Sahib Jee by grinding down sandalwood and saffron (to apply them as perfumes), lighting incense and offering flowers.
(Sri Gur Partap Suraj Granth, Page 2140)

6. Sri Guru Har Gobind Sahib Jee

The warrior Guru, the vanquisher of armies, is very brave and benevolent.
(Bhai Gurdas Jee, Var 1, Pauri 48)

After gaining victory in the battle of Hargobindpur Sahib, the Sixth Satguru, Sri Guru Hargobind Jee, listened to the recitation of Jap Jee Sahib from Bhai Gopala Jee. Bhai Gopala Jee was seated on a platform higher than Guru Jee's own throne (out of respect for Gurbani as he was reading Gurbani). Upon hearing such a pristine pronunciation of Jap Jee Sahib from Bhai Gopala Jee, Satguru Jee was prepared to bestow the Guruship upon him.

Mata Damodari Jee's sister, Bibi Ramo Jee and her husband Bhai Saee Das Jee, remembered and meditated

96

upon Guru Sahib with great respect and affection; for this reason, Satguru Jee prepared to visit them at their village, Daroali. On reaching Sachkhand Sri Harimandar Sahib, Guru Sahib performed the Ardaas, circumbulated around Sri Harimandar Sahib four times and then went to Sri Akaal Takhat Sahib. Satguru Jee seated Sri Guru Granth Sahib Jee on a beautiful throne at the front of the procession. Then Guru Sahib Jee followed gracefully and respectfully, along with the rest of the Sangat and made Their way to the village.

7. Sri Guru Har Rai Jee

Sangat from a faraway country came singing Kirtan towards the lotus feet of the Seventh King, Sri Guru Har Rai Jee. When the Sangat got very close, Guru Sahib Jee got up very quickly from Their throne, hitting Their knee against the side of Their throne, thus causing Themselves an injury (in order to maintain respect for Gurbani). When the shocked Sangat asked, "Maharaj, why did you arise in such a rush?" Guru Sahib Jee replied, "O' Brothers! The Sangat was reciting Gurbani. We arose so quickly out of respect for Gurbani. If we falter from respecting Gurbani, how can we expect others to respect Gurbani?" Satguru Jee blessed the Sangat with the following Divine Words:

Any Sikh who fears Gurbani will cross this world ocean
without any effort|...||15||
The one who is lovingly devoted to the Guru is my Sikh
and has great awe and respect for Gurbani.
The person who has no fear or respect of
Gurbani is not my Sikh. ||20||
(Sri Gur Partap Suraj Granth, Page 3344 – 45)

97

The Seventh King's highly intelligent Sahibzada, Sri Ram Rai Jee, was graced with the blessing by Guru Sahib Jee that "We (Guru Sahib Jee) will abide on your tongue, and whatever you say will come true". This boon came true and Ram Rai Jee showed great miracles in the court of Aurangzeb. Every day, 13,000 Rupees would come to Ram Rai Jee's headquarters, courtesy of Emperor Aurangzeb. However, when Ram Rai Jee changed the line *"Soil is of the Muslim"* to "Soil is of those that are fraudulent". (This line is from Sri Guru Nanak Dev Jee's Asa Raag Ang 466 and is talking of when Muslims are buried their bodies disintegrate into the soil) Satguru Har Rai Sahib Jee was extremely offended and disappointed - They told Ram Rai that They did not wish to even see someone who had altered Gurbani of the most respected Satguru (Sri Guru Nanak Dev Jee), and had altered the word of God. Ram Rai was ordered to continue to walk in whichever direction he was facing, and to never return. It was also ordered that no Sikh should worship or acknowledge Ram Rai. In this way, he was excommunicated from the house of the Guru.

8. Sri Guru Har Krishan Jee

When the Eighth King, Sri Guru Har Krishan Jee, went to Delhi, Emperor Aurangzeb asked to see Them. The True King wrote down the following:

What good is food, and what good are clothes?
(Sri Guru Granth Sahib Jee, Ang 142)

Guru Sahib Jee sent this to Aurangzeb as a message that the true Darshan of the King of Kings was within the Shabad, which should reside within one's heart.

9. Sri Guru Tegh Bahadur Jee

Sri Guru Tegh Bahadur Sahib Jee went to visit Prayagraj Tribeni (today this is the city of Prayagraj). At that place, Guru Sahib Jee's respected Mother, Mata Nanaki Jee, requested to have the sight of a Grandson. Guru Sahib Jee said, "Carry out an Akhand Paath of Sri Guru Granth Sahib Jee and God will most definitely fulfil your request."

In the Dharam Vijai Shastar (an ancient text), it is written that the Akhand Paath Sahib was conducted from the Saroop of Sri Guru Granth Sahib (compiled by Bhai Banno Jee). The Akhand Paath Sahib was conducted by Guru Sahib Jee, at the site of 'Vadee Sikh Sangat Gurdwara' in Prayagraj. These five Sikhs were the Paathis (reciters) of the Akhand Paath,

1. Bhai Mati Das Jee
2. Bhai Dayala Jee
3. Bhai Gurbaksh Singh Jee Masand
4. Bhai Gurdita Jee, (who was the 6th descendant in the lineage of Baba Budha Sahib Jee)
5. Bhai Sati Ram Jee (who was a Sikh of the Eighth King)

The Ninth King blessed these five Sikhs with the responsibility to carry out the Akhand Paath for the arrival of Sri Guru Gobind Singh Jee. Only after the completion of this Akhand Paath did Sri Guru Gobind Singh Jee arrive:

There (in Allahabad) I was conceived (March 1666 CE).
Later, I took birth at Patna (December 1666 CE)
(Sri Dasam Granth Sahib Jee, Ang 59)

10. Sri Guru Gobind Singh Jee

In Anandpur Sahib, the Tenth King punished a Singh for pronouncing a vowel of Gurmukhi incorrectly. Guru Jee said, "O' Singh! You have just broken my limbs!" Subsequently, at Guru Ki Kaanshi (Sri Damdama Sahib), Guru Jee gave the knowledge of correct pronunciation and meanings of Gurbani. The Chief Poet, Bhai Nand Lal Singh Jee humbly asked Guru Jee, "Oh Great King, where can we have your blessed vision (Darshan)?"

The words of Bhai Nand Laal Singh Jee.
Gurdev Jee (my benefactor Guru), you have commanded us (the Sikhs), to have Your Darshan (blessed sight). How can all Sikhs have your Darshan (because some Sikhs may live miles away)? Please explain this to me.
The divine words of the Respected Guru.
I have three forms; listen O' Nand Lal! Whilst focusing with all your concentration. Without attributes (Nirgun), with attributes (Sargun) and the divine word of the Guru (Gurshabad), I say this to make you understand (that these are the three forms of the Guru).

Three days prior to their ascension to Sachkhand, the True Father, Sri Guru Gobind Singh Jee Maharaj, gave the Eternal Guruship to the Spiritual Light of the Ten Gurus, Sri Guru Granth Sahib Jee, with their own hands. Guru Sahib Jee made Sri Guru Granth Sahib Jee the Master of the Chaur (fan), Chhattar (royal canopy) and Takhat (royal throne) for eternity and put the whole world under the protection and guidance of Sri Guru Granth Sahib Jee and gave the following command:

The Great Timeless Lord commanded me to create and start this Nation.

It is a commandment that all Sikhs are to accept Sri Guru Granth Sahib Jee as their Guru.

In Their ten forms, the Gurus upheld the respect, love and fear of Gurbani. We should continue to uphold this respect of Gurbani as Satguru Jee did. In order to show the utmost respect to Gurbani, there are certain rules which must be adhered to:

- You should not sit on Guru Jee's Tabiya (platform), without having bathed and washed your feet.

- When the body has become impure or unclean due to sexual activity, one should wash their hair, wear clean clothes, recite Jap Jee Sahib and perform Ardaas before sitting on Tabiya.

- If you touch your face, feet, kachhera, moustache, have an itch or have wet or dirty hands then you should not touch Sri Guru Granth Sahib Jee, Pothia or Gutke.

- Whilst sitting on Tabiya, you must not eat or put anything in your mouth.

- A person sitting on Guru Jee's Tabiya must sit upright in a cross-legged position, without any pillows for support and must not rest their elbows on the Manji Sahib.

- He should always sit unaided and behind the Manji Sahib (he must ensure that his legs are not under the Manji Sahib).

We must respect and accept Guru Jee's Command with the full faith that Sri Guru Granth Sahib Jee is seated before us and is the Spiritual Light of our Ten Satguru Jees. We should recognise and accept the Bani from *the first Ang through* to *the 1430 Ang, including Raagmala* as Gurbani, the Eternal Guru.[80]

Maharaj Sahib, the Respected King, should never be placed or kept in a cupboard, wardrobe or trunk; instead, They should be kept in a clean, airy room which should house a palanquin for Them to be seated upon. The throne (Palki), where Guru Jee takes Their seat during the day, should be spacious and should contain a small canopy and, above that, there must be a bigger canopy because Satguru Jee is the King of the Chaur, Chhattar and Takhat (royal fan, canopy and throne).

---

[80] Raagmala was authored by Guru Jee. Sri Guru Arjan Dev Jee Maharaj got Bhai Gurdas Jee to write the first Saroop of Aad Sri Guru Granth Sahib Jee – in which Raagmala is present; it is written in the same ink, on the same quality paper and in the same handwriting as the rest of the Gurbani. This Saroop is now at Sri Kartarpur Sahib, (Doaba). Whosoever doubts Raagmala can check this Saroop. Bhai Banno Jee prepared a copy of this Saroop, which also includes Raagmala. At Takhat Sri Damdama Sahib, Sri Guru Gobind Singh Jee Maharaj, got Bhai Mani Singh Jee to be scribe whilst Guru Jee recited the whole of Sri Guru Granth Sahib Jee, in which Raagmala is present. It is also present in the 4 Saroops written by Shaheed Baba Deep Singh Jee. Those that argue that the poet Jodh wrote Raagmala in 'Madavanal Kamkandla' or that the poet Aalam wrote it are in actual fact, mistaken. The poet Jodh wrote 'Madavanal Kamkandla' in Sanskrit in the Hijra year 991 (Muslim calendar), which is 1640 Bikrami (1583 CE) in which Raagmala is not present. The poet Aalam was one of Satguru Sri Guru Gobind Singh Jee's 52 poets; he lived from 1712 Bikrami (1655 CE) to 1774 Bikrami (1717 CE). He wrote the Raagmala according to what he heard spoken in the court of Sri Guru Gobind Singh Jee. The poet Aalam lived 113 years after the first Saroop of Sri Guru Granth Sahib Jee was compiled – how could anyone argue that Aalam authored Raagmala 113 years after the compilation of the first Saroop of Sri Guru Granth Sahib Jee? From this it is clear that Guru Sahib authored Raagmala. Dr. Veer Singh Jee explains in depth that Guru Jee authored Raagmala in Sri Gurpartap Suraj Granth from Panna 2128 to Panna 2133. If one were to read Giani Sahib Singh's (Dhamdhaan Sahib), detailed discourse about the authenticity of Raagmala, no confusion and doubt would be left and one would surely be convinced that Raagmala was written by Guru Jee and that it is Gurbani. For these reasons each and every Gursikh should accept Raagmala as Gurbani without any doubts. For those who would like to read about Raagmala in more depth and detail please read the small book called "Raagmala Gurbani Hai", published by Damdami Taksal. (This book contains the spiritual meaning of Raagmala and has arguments for any point that has ever been raised against Raagmala's authenticity)

Guru Arjan Dev Jee sits on the throne;
the royal canopy waves over the True Guru.
(Sri Guru Granth Sahib Jee, Ang 968)

Wherever Sri Guru Granth Sahib Jee is Parkash or in Sukhaasan, no one should sit on a chair or platform in front of Guru Sahib Jee - everyone should sit on the floor with a sheet beneath them, if needed.

Let yourselves be joined to the Name of the Lord;
become Gurmukh, spread out your mat, and sit down.
(Sri Guru Granth Sahib Jee, Ang 1185)

Whenever you see Satguru Sri Guru Granth Sahib Jee, or whenever you see Guru Jee's Sangat reciting or singing Gurbani Kirtan, you should take off your shoes and place your hands together, stand with respect and bow. For however long Sri Guru Granth Sahib Jee is present, you should stand in respect. Whenever Guru Jee is travelling, there should be five Singhs alongside them. The Singhs should walk barefoot, without any shoes or sandals. One Singh should wave the Chaur Sahib over Guru Jee, and one should walk before Guru Jee who should be purifying the path before them by splashing water. If Guru Jee is to be seated in a car then the water should be taken along with them.

If you are to recite Gurbani from a Pothi Sahib or Gutka Sahib then a sheet should be placed down in order for you to sit on. If there is a bed or chair, you should recite the Gurbani sitting on the highest seat.

Every time you have a Gutka Sahib in your hands, you should also always have a Rumala Sahib to cover it. Whenever you use a Pothi Sahib for Kirtan or Gutka Sahib for Nitnem or to read any Bani, it is highly important to always keep a Rumala Sahib with the Gutka or Pothi Sahib. If you are reciting Gurbani or reading from a Gutka Sahib and there is another person sitting on a higher platform than you, you should not: face their feet, sit lower than them or on the floor, or sit behind them. Should someone wish to learn Santhia (correct pronunciation of Gurbani) then the teacher should not sit at a higher level than the student (unless they both have Pothi Sahibs in front of them; in this situation, they would sit at the same level).

All scriptures of Gurbani, whether they be Gutke Sahibs, Sri Dasam Granth Sahib Jee, Bhai Gurdas Jee's Bani and any other scriptures that are Gurmat based, should be shown the utmost respect at all times. Any other books should be kept separate and Gurbani or Gurmat related scriptures should be kept in a higher place. The Pothi or Gutka Sahib should be clothed with clean, fresh Rumala Sahibs (which are made to fit them) and kept respectfully closed in a high clean place on the same side as your pillow (if in your bedroom so your feet are not in Their direction when you sleep/lay down).

On many occasions it has been known that some people keep a small Gutka Sahib in their pocket, leather purse or bag for when they are travelling on buses or in cars, etc. Without thinking about their Joothe (unclean) hands, they begin to recite Gurbani with their shoes and socks on – this a huge mistake and very disrespectful. In these instances, you should recite Gurbani that you have memorised or simply repeat Gurmantar 'Vaheguru'. It is not acceptable to begin to read from a Pothi or Gutka Sahib whilst wearing shoes or sandals and without having your head and body covered.

If a Gutka Sahib or Pothi Sahib is to be kept in a trunk or cupboard, then it must be kept in a clean state without any dirty clothes, shoes or Kachheras. When keeping Gutka Sahibs or Pothi Sahibs in the house, they should be kept in a clean place which is high and away from where you will point your feet (i.e. near your pillow – if in your bedroom). They should be kept in decorative Rumalas and each Gutka or Pothi Sahib should have its own Rumala and should not be in a position where feet can be directed towards them, nor should you turn your back to that place.

Within Sri Guru Granth Sahib Jee, or any Gutka or Pothi Sahib, there should be no pieces of paper or thread to act as a bookmark. When the Paathi Singh is reciting Paath, he should remember to turn the Ang with his right hand from the top of the Ang and should not use his left hand from the bottom (this is to ensure respect of the Angs and this method reduces the Ang on the right hand-side getting worn at the edges). Whenever doing Paath, you should never put your feet underneath Satguru Jee's Manji Sahib and you should always sit back from the Manji Sahib and remain sitting upright with legs crossed. Your knees should never be bent so that you are sitting on them nor should they be raised (it is important to remain sitting in a cross-legged position). Also, if a Singh or a Kaur is performing Katha in the Hazoori of Guru Sahib Jee, he/she should keep the limbs of his body under control – he/she should not raise his/her hands higher than Guru Sahib or make inappropriate hand movements in order to explain something to the Sangat.

When reading from Sri Guru Granth Sahib Jee, you should not keep your hands or fingers placed on the Angs. If there is a breeze coming through the room then place the Rumala Sahib over Guru Jee and then hold down the Ang -

you should not keep your hands or fingers over the Angs without a Rumala.

Red or green Rumalas, or Rumalas with pictures on them, should not be placed over Guru Jee (the colour prohibitions are in line with the Khalsa colours explained earlier in the code of conduct). Instead, beautiful and expensive Rumalas should be washed and then offered to Guru Sahib Jee. They should be large and should fit the Manji Sahib with ease. The Chaur Sahib should be waved over Satguru Jee and if you wish to apply perfume then apply it only to the Rumalas, not on the Angs directly. You should endeavor to have flowers present as well as dhooph (incense), and a jot (lantern made from Desi Ghee). Lanterns that burn gas should not be used to provide light in the Hazoori of Sri Guru Granth Sahib Jee.

At any time when a Gursikh is listening to Gurbani through a radio, tape cassette, CD or television, the form of communication should be placed higher than those that are listening in order to maintain the respect of Gurbani. If Gurbani appears in newspapers, letters, sweet boxes, books or wedding cards, these should not be thrown away or allowed to be placed amongst rubbish or near the feet. If you are unable to keep or look after them then they must be placed in a fire, following the Maryada of Agan Bhet (in which you carefully cremate the Gurbani, keep the ashes and disperse them in flowing water, stream, river or ocean).

If you have been to the bathroom or have been outside where someone has been smoking and your clothes have become unclean due to the smoke, then do not sit at Guru Jee's Tabiya. You should bathe and change into clean clothes, or wash your existing clothes and wait for them to dry before sitting at Guru Jee's Tabiya.

Whilst wearing a Choti Dastar (Keski), or a Patka, you should not sit at Guru Jee's Tabiya; instead, you should tie a full Dastar (a full dastar consists of a Keski/Choti Dastar underneath with a larger Dastar on top) and then proceed into Guru Jee's Darbar. Women should never sit at Guru Jee's Tabiya whilst wearing jewellery, bindis or make-up, such as lipstick. They should wear pale coloured, clean, simple clothes and must always keep their head completely covered – with an appropriate head covering that does not keep slipping. Women who are menstruating should not sit at Sri Guru Granth Sahib Jee's Tabiya, nor should they do Chaur Sahib seva.

Kaviraj (poet) Sant Nihal Singh Jee tells us about the code of conduct regarding Paath:

The conduct regarding Paath (before going onto Sri Guru Granth Sahib Jee's Tabiya): make sure you eat little. Whilst sitting on Sri Guru Granth Sahib Jee's Tabiya, sit with your legs crossed; keep the volume and tone of your voice under control and recite Gurbani in one clear tone.
Keep your consciousness focused, and read with loving devotion; do not place a pillow under yourself and do not rest your hands on Sri Guru Granth Sahib Jee's Manji Sahib. From Sri Guru Granth Sahib Jee's Tabiya do not cough, and do not say any angry words, do not yawn, do not burp, do not sneeze, do not laugh, do not clean your nose, do not produce flatulence and do not spit. With a peaceful nature, and focusing on the Immortal Lord; O Beloved ones! In such a way recite Gurbani from Sri Guru Granth Sahib Jee Maharaj.
(Gurmat Maartandd, Second Section, Panna 421)

After going to the toilet, washing your hands five times with soap, sand or soil is a bare minimum (this is for when you are about to handle Gurbani in order to ensure the utmost hygiene). Even after passing urine, it is required for you to wash your hands. If your hands have come into contact with shoes then you are required to wash your hands twice; if soil or sand is unavailable as a detergent then soap is acceptable. You must wash your hands thoroughly and then dry them with a cloth before coming into contact with Gurbani. When washing your hands, make sure that you wash your hands completely and thoroughly (starting from the fingers and going all the way up to, and including, the wrist) as some people tend to just wet their fingers – this is unacceptable.

Some shopkeepers do Parkash of Gutka Sahibs and read Gurbani whilst they are running the shop; as soon as a customer arrives, they put the Gutka Sahib down on the (joothee) unclean counter and begin to serve the customer. As soon as the customer leaves, they do not wash their hands and pick up the Gutka Sahib with (joothe) unclean hands and continue to read – this is a huge mistake and very disrespectful. For this reason, it is advised that whilst you are working you should recite Gurbani from memory, or if not, simply repeat Gurmantar (the word Vaheguru).

The cleaning of your teeth is paramount, every day (Puratan Singhs used to use daatan to clean their teeth – this method is still used in Sampardas, such as Damdami Taksal, Nihang Singhs, etc). If you do not have access to daatan then using toothpaste is acceptable. If you use daatan, tear it and throw it away after using it.

It is important that you have the utmost respect for Shastar (weapons) as well. Do not place your feet in the direction of Shastar. You should not place your faith in, or bow to, anyone other than Sri Guru Granth Sahib Jee or Gurbani.

The Khalsa meditates on the Ever-radiant Light of God, day and night, rejecting all else but the one Lord from his mind.He decorates himself with perfect love and faith, and does not believe in adhering to fasts, or worshipping tombs, crematoriums and graves, even by mistake.
Acts of pilgrimage, charity, compassion, austerities and superstitious self-control are to no avail if one does not recognize the One Lord God.
Such a being, in whose heart shines the full Divinely Radiant Light is truly a pure Khalsa, others are false.
(Sri Dasam Granth Sahib Jee, Ang 712)

Do not eat the parshaad or any other food from a Peer Fakeer's tomb, Marree (tombs), Gugga (snake worshippers) or Mata Rani (goddess worshippers) because whoever eats parshaad from such places (as mentioned above) is not at all a Sikh.

Do not have lewd photos inside your house. Display pictures of great warriors, saints, and of the True Gurus but do not point your feet towards these photos. At the Gurdwara, or if Sri Guru Granth Sahib Jee are present within the home, do not display pictures in front of Them. Pictures in which people are wearing shoes must not be displayed in front of Guru Jee as it is a grave sin.

In small villages, many people used cow dung as a floor cover on the floors in the kitchen area. The area in which Sri Guru Granth Sahib Jee's Parkash is to be done should never have such floor covering because the cow dung is both unclean and foul smelling.

Amritdhari women are forbidden from participating in teeya (a day where all the ladies of a village would get together and dance), nor should they indulge in bhangra or gidha (neither should the men as these practices are condemned in Gurbani and in the code of conduct).

The Khalsa should remain alert and stay away from anyone who sits on a raised platform or on a pillow in Sri Guru Granth Sahib Jee's blessed Hazoori (presence), or anyone who allows people to bow before them in Guru Jee's Hazoori or practices black magic.

Just as a Gursikh is required to take 10% of their earnings and donate them to the Gurdwara, in the same way, out of 24 hours a Gursikh is required to take two and a half hours out for Simran. It is compulsory for a Gursikh to memorise the names of the ten Guru Sahib Jees, five Beloved Gursikhs that were first blessed with Khande-Batte-da-Amrit (Panj Pyare), four sons of Sri Guru Gobind Singh Jee (Sahibzaday), and the five Highest Thrones (Panj Takhat Sahib).

In many homes there are Saroops of Sri Guru Granth Sahib Jee, however, even the Parkash Seva of these Saroops is not done, hence there is a lot of disrespect of these Saroops. The Parkash, respect and worship of these Saroops should certainly take place. Those people who keep Satguru Jee's Saroops at home, but do not respect them fully, are committing a grave sin. Those people should respectfully take the Saroops of Satguru Jee to a place where the respect of Satguru Jee is upheld. Some people believe they lose everything by taking Satguru Jee from their homes to a place of respect; this, however, is not the case. In fact by taking Satguru Jee to a place of respect, they will be blessed with a great reward. According to the Maryada created by our Satgurus, it is imperative to upkeep the utmost respect of Sri Guru Granth Sahib Jee.

Satguru Amar Das Jee's daughter, Bibi Bhaani Jee, was an embodiment of loving devotion. The story of how Bibi Jee placed her hand under the broken leg of the chair of her father and how the wood pierced through her hand is well known; and it shows how much respect Bibi Jee had for Guru Jee. For this reason, wherever there is a devoted Gursikh Parcharak (preacher), he or she should uphold the respect for Sri Guru Granth Sahib Jee by spreading the message throughout his or her local area and wherever he or she may go.

Inside the Gurdwara Sahib, incense sticks, candles and ghee lamps, etc, should be kept in a case, which either has wire mesh or glass around the outside. Many times foolish people light incense sticks or candles and then leave. Many fires have been started due to this reason. Indeed incense should be lit both in the morning and evening, however, the incense sticks or ghee lamps should be placed away from the Rumalas. These should only be lit as long as a Sevadar is present, otherwise they could become fire hazards; for this reason, devoted servants of Guru Jee must be aware.

Sometimes the ghee from the ghee lamps spills onto the Angs of Sri Guru Granth Sahib Jee and mice come and gnaw away at the spoiled Angs. Some foolish people put candles directly above the Angs whilst they read and so wax melts and falls onto the Angs, which spoils them. This is a terrible sin - may Maharaj Jee save us from such sins.

At many places, flowers placed in front of Sri Guru Granth Sahib Jee catch fire due to the waving of ghee lamps in a plate during Aartee. For this reason, ghee lamps should not be lit during Aartee. Satguru Jee has recited the Shabads for the Aartee, therefore, only the Kirtan of these Shabads should be performed.

111

Some people lie down with their feet towards Sri Guru Granth Sahib Jee or the Gurdwara Sahib. If you tell them this is wrong, they reply with, "God is in all four directions." You should never cite the example of the form of God, Sri Guru Nanak Dev Jee, in order to justify lying down with your feet facing towards a religious place of worship of any religion or Sri Guru Granth Sahib Jee. When Guru Sahib Jee used to go outside, the Sikhs who were on guard duty used to run in front of Them; if anyone was lying down with their feet facing towards the path of Guru Jee, the Sikhs would wake them up and say, "Wake up O' brother! Be alert, cover your head, bow down and be blessed with great fortunes." The person sleeping would become ecstatic and say, "Thank you for waking me up and blessing me with the Darshan of Guru Sahib Jee."

Shopkeepers should give full guidance about the worship and respect of religious scriptures to customers. Sometimes, out of greed, shopkeepers do not even tell customers, 'First wash your hands, then have Darshan,' before viewing blessed Saroops of Sri Guru Granth Sahib Jee or religious scriptures.

Most cassettes and CDs have mispronounced Gurbani recorded on them. Instead of listening to a cassette or CD of Nitnem, it is better to read Nitnem yourself. When we read Gurbani to Sri Guru Granth Sahib Jee and to the Sangat, then Maharaj Jee becomes pleased with us. Most people turn on cassettes and CDs whilst lying on their beds. There was already a lot of laziness but, with this, it has increased even more. Due to this, people have stopped learning the Shudh Santhia (correct pronunciation of Gurbani). For this reason, it is an urgent request to all to learn Shudh Santhia and read correctly pronounced (Shudh) Gurbani to Guru Sahib and the Sangat in order to receive Their blessings. Only Gurbani recordings that are Shudh should be listened to; by doing so, you can learn how to read Gurbani correctly. Also, we humbly request that those people, who record Gurbani, to take full care that Gurbani is recorded correctly.

O readers,

> *The Creator Lord is our only friend.*
> (Sri Guru Granth Sahib Jee, Ang 692)

Saroops, Gutkas, Pothis and religious literature containing Gurbani from the Perfect Embodiment of the Creator Lord, Sri Guru Granth Sahib Jee, should be lovingly printed correctly on the best paper possible, and should be respectfully kept in the best Rumalas possible.

Sri Guru Granth Sahib Jee is the revered Satguru of all. No one should launch an attack on the respected Saroops of Satguru Sahib Jee, or on any Gurdwaras. Those evil egotistical people who carry out such disrespect are hacking away at themselves with the axe of evil. To attack someone in the Hazoori of Guru Jee, or someone who is reading Gurbani anywhere, is also a terrible sin.

May Sri Guru Granth Sahib Jee bless the Panth with such determination that there is a high level of organisation in which a list is made of all the divine and respected Saroops of Guru Jee in the world. In each area there should be groups of people who get together and make sure that the respect and honour of the divine and respected Saroops of Guru Jee and Gurdwaras are upheld. Every Sikh should up hold respect of Satguru Jee himself or herself and should make sure others uphold this as well. Those who do not keep the respect of Guru Jee should be subjected to a punishment (tankhaah) - this will mean that everyone will remain vigilant and maintain respect.

In houses, the Parkash or accommodation of Sri Guru Granth Sahib Jee, should not take place under stairs or in a tight confined space. In this way there is terrible disrespect and a lot of sins are accumulated. For this reason, any brothers or sisters, who want to have Sri Guru Granth Sahib Jee's divine presence (Parkash) in their homes, must ensure they have a beautiful, clean well ventilated room available.

You should cover the heads and remove shoes of small children before they enter the presence (hazoori) of Satguru Jee.

Those fakes who indulge in black magic, the harnessing of ghosts as well as other such anti-gurmat activities whilst keeping Saroops of Sri Guru Granth Sahib Jee, should be banned from doing so in accordance to the command of the Khalsa Panth. When we do not want to go to such places ourselves, why are Saroops of Sri Guru Granth Sahib Jee taken and kept at such places?

At some places, fake preachers sit on the same level as Sri Guru Granth Sahib Jee, with a canopy above themselves, and get people to worship them; they are afflicted by the heinous sin due to disrespecting Satguru Jee.

The numbers that are used for counting lines in Gurbani should not be pronounced. By pronouncing these numbers, the Gurbani recitation is broken. Also, the concentration of those listening is broken. Those listening to the Gurbani cannot focus. According to Guru Jee's code of conduct (Maryada), the numbers counting up Astpadis, Shabads, etc, should not be recited.

Someone, who is reading from a Pothi Sahib or Gutka Sahib, should lay down a cloth under where he or she is sitting and a separate cloth under the wooden stand on which the Pothi or Gutka Sahib is placed. The cloth that is laid under the Pothi or Gutka Sahib should be higher than the one lying under the reader. You should not read a Pothi or Gutka Sahib on the bare floor, without laying anything on the ground.

That table upon which religious scriptures are placed should not be dragged. Respectfully pick up the religious scriptures - if you pick up the table with the religious scriptures still upon it, make sure that the table does not topple over.

When removing the Pothi at the bottom of a pile of Pothis, please first respectfully bow and remove the Pothis on top. Then respectfully remove the Pothi from the bottom of the pile. If you try and pull the Pothi at the bottom of the pile, the Pothis on top could fall over.

There are many Gurdwaras that are without Granthi Singhs due to the lack of pay as well as petty politics; Gurmukhs blessed with these skills rarely take on this Seva. In the old days, there were few Gurdwaras and they were less grand, however, the feeling of Gursikhi was abundant in them. Nowadays, the Gurdwaras are lavish but also ravaged by petty politics and personal agenda; unfortunately, the sentiments of Gursikhi and Seva are decreasing day by day. Because there is more than one Gurdwara in virtually every village, we are not fully respecting Sri Guru Granth Sahib Jee or Granthi Singhs. In many places there is not even a separate room made for the

Sukhasan Seva of Guru Jee. In the summer, a fan is not turned on and in winter blankets are not offered. Pigeons and other animals are allowed to make noise and mess, thus disrespecting Guru Jee. Many people believe Granthis to be useless and idle; Granthi Singhs will only stay where there is love and respect. For this reason, that person who has taken Shudh Santhia of Aad Sri Guru Granth Sahib Jee with full attention to all consonants and vowels, his or her pay should be generous according to the economic conditions that exist at that time. This will mean that the Gurmukh Sikh can focus on reading Gurbani Shudh, learning meanings and Sikh history and commit himself or herself totally to the true service of Guru Sahib Jee. This will really help spread the message of Sikhi. For example, if 200 households gave 2000 rupees as a monthly wage - this would only mean 10 rupees a month from each house. (In line with inflation now the wage would have to be more in India too, this figure is taken from when the original publication went to print). Wherever Sant Baba Gurbachan Singh Jee 'Khalsa' Bhindranwale travelled with their Jatha, in those places the Sangat fully respected the Granthi Singhs as these teachings were enshrined in those villages and cities.

The Granthi Singh should carry out his Seva with love to receive the blessings of Sri Guru Nanak Dev Jee even if wages are low because:

One, who performs selfless service without thought of reward, shall attain his Lord and Master.
(Sri Guru Granth Sahib Jee, Ang 286)

Even if someone speaks harshly to him, he should consider himself a servant of the Guru and carry out his duty happily. He should be humble, kind and loving to all. He should not be lazy and sleep all the time; such a pleasure ends up becoming a disease. Those great souls who have done Seva are immortal forever. To this day, there are institutions that flourish in their name (like Bhai Ghanaiya Jee who kept healing and giving water to all the soldiers in the midst of battle). When the next Mahapurakh (great soul) takes charge of this Samparda (institution) started by Bhai Ghanaiya Jee, he is given a broom, a box of healing balm and a pitcher; the broom is for sweeping the house of the Guru, the box of healing balm is to heal people for free and the pitcher is to welcome all and offer them food and water, which symbolises dying on a worldly level in order to perform true selfless service.

It is the duty of the Granthi Singh to read Nitnem and the Sri Mukhvak to the congregation in the morning and evening and to teach children (Shudh Santhia) accurate pronunciation of Gurbani. He should look after Pothi Sahibs and distribute and collect them in from the Sangat in order for the Sangat to read them. He should remove any dust from the blessed Angs of Sri Guru Granth Sahib Jee. He should perform the Seva of conducting Katha (religious sermons) and Kirtan. He should encourage the Sangat to visit important religious places and to give up using any intoxicants. He should happily carry out Seva without any desires and should spread the message of righteousness (Dharam).

We humbly ask all beloved readers to help your local Granthi Singh as much as you can. Whilst Parkash and Sukhasan Seva are being performed, you can wave the Chaur Sahib above Sri Guru Granth Sahib Jee. Do not think "Why should we do the Seva? This is just the duty of the Granthi Singh." One person alone cannot carry out complete Seva with full respect - when the whole Sangat carries out the Seva with true devotion then it is true Seva. Seeing the love of the Sangat, the Granthi Singh's love

117

increases and, seeing the love of the Granthi Singh, the Sangat's love increases. Sri Guru Granth Sahib Jee protects us in this world and the next. Beloved Gursikhs should lovingly, and with full respect, unite with the Granthi Singh to carry out the Seva of Guru Jee. The Granthi Singh should also lovingly spread the message and encourage the Sangat to join in with the Seva. He should remain alert that they are taking part in all the Seva and he, too, should do the Seva as well. The Granthi Singh should take no part in politics. Wherever he hears slander, he should leave it there; he should never indulge in slander. He should consider himself the slave of Guru Nanak Sahib, and should consider it in his own welfare to bring an end to politics.

Granthi Singhs who teach the true pronunciation of Gurbani, Katha and Kirtan are very rare. To such Gurmukhs, we humbly bow again and again. By serving and respecting those Granthi Singhs, the whole Sangat should take the benefit of the (Shudh Santhia) correct pronunciation of Gurbani, Katha and Kirtan.

At many places arguments arise regarding loud speakers (being used in villages or publicly relaying the Gurdwara program, mainly relevant in India). It is argued that the use of loud speakers are detrimental to the education of children and do not let people sleep at night. However, if lewd songs are played, no one tries to stop them (when people have parties and weddings). At many places, due to these arguments, the Amrit Vela Nitnem is done later in the morning. In reality we should have faith ourselves and encourage faith in the children. By listening to Gurbani, the children's moral character develops, therefore, the children are saved from the use of intoxicants. If the ears hear the sweet sound of Gurbani, then the ears are blessed and the mind becomes calm and peaceful. With a calm mind, worldly education is also more easily performed. We also make the mistake of saying, "Gurbani entering our ears will mean we cannot go to sleep." In fact, listening to the ambrosial Katha, Kirtan and recitation of Gurbani calms the mind: thinking, anxieties, stresses are all removed, the mind becomes tranquil and sleep comes naturally.

Gutkas and Pothis of Gurbani and Rumalas for Sri Guru Granth Sahib that are kept in trunks or wardrobes, and the beds for Guru Sahib, should be kept with mothballs, etc, so that insects do not ruin them. Blessed Saroops, Gutkas and Pothis should be carefully kept away from damp as well. Gutkas and Pothis should not be kept in wardrobes that are built into walls because damp can arise through them and affect the Gutkas and Pothis. At least every 6 months, the Pothis should be aired and perfumed with incense. Due to neglect and damp, etc, many important Pothis have been lost. After the passing away of a Sant or a Giani Singh, special care should be taken in looking after the Pothis.

It is a great disrespect of Guru Sahib to make Rumalas containing pictures of Guru Sahib or lines of Gurbani. Only those Rumalas should be presented to Guru Sahib Jee which do not have lines from Gurbani written on them because Rumalas are offered out of respect for Gurbani. Although, if Gurbani is written on the Rumalas then dust and dirt will fall upon them.

Those cassettes, records and CDs which have Gurbani on them should be respected like Pothis - when they break, they should not be left to waste away beneath our feet.

Phones and electronic devices such as tablets and anything else that you read Gurbani off should be sanitized before use and where possible Gutka Sahibs used instead. Sanitization should preferably be done with alcohol free products and only carried out on electronic devices and never on Gutka Sahibs. Gutkas and Gurbani pothia should be wiped down regularly to keep them dust free but no wet applications of cleaning are needed for them.

Every month you should take a soft cloth and clean each Ang of Sri Guru Granth Sahib Jee to remove any dust. Do not press down the cloth too hard because the ink in some Saroops may run. Even the hand should not be pressed against the Angs as the hand is sweaty and dirty.

Young children copy the elders and start waving the Chaur Sahib, however, they do not know about washing their hands and feet and they do not know about the respect required. For this reason, one Sikh should remain on guard with Guru Sahib whilst reciting Gurbani (children are allowed to do the seva but should be adequately supervised and/or trained).

If one person is sitting behind Sri Guru Granth Sahib Jee on Tabiyaa then make sure to pass Pothis in front of this person – not behind them. If someone is standing beside a table on which Pothi Sahibs are rested then you should not hand out or return a Pothi behind their back. Nothing should be passed over the top of Guru Sahib Jee or a Gutka Sahib or Pothi Sahib. When sitting on your bed, pass Pothi Sahibs over the side of the pillow. We should not be sitting on the side of the pillow and passing the Pothi Sahib over the side where our feet usually lie (your head is the supreme point of your body and it rests on the pillow at night. This is why it is referred to so often here in these descriptions).

If one person is reading from a Gutka Sahib or a Pothi Sahib then another person should not start reading a Gutka Sahib back to back with that person as is now commonly seen in many Gurdwara Sahibs. In this way, both have their backs facing towards Gurbani.

If you are practising Kirtan on your bed then place the instrument on the side of your pillow. The cloths of the instrument should not touch your feet. Do not place the Amrit Kirtan Pothi Sahib on the instrument without a Rumala and do not commit the sin of placing keys, money, etc, or anything on top of the Pothi Sahib.

Some people keep their hands in the middle of the Pothi Sahibs whilst reading from it, and needlessly keep turning over the Angs of the Pothi Sahib - doing so can make the Angs dirty, thus causes them to rip. If your Pothis or Gutka Sahibs become torn, the best way to repair them is by using starch paste and a good quality paper which is thin enough to blend in.[81] Using any form of tape to repair Pothis or Gutka Sahibs causes the paper to degrade.

Whilst reading from a Pothi Sahib or Gutka Sahib, you should not allow a fly or any other insect to rest upon it. Sometimes seeing a creature on the Ang, we act in haste and squash the animal into the Ang. We should feel mercy towards the creature and move it away gently with a piece of cloth.

You should never say disrespectful words like Paath-Pooth, Pothi-Paathi, Nitnem-Nitnoom, Baani-Booni, Gutka-Gatka, Kirtan-Koortan, etc. Whilst reading from a Gutka Sahib or Pothi Sahib, some people leave the Gutka

---

[81] For further advice on making such repairs, please contact pothiseva@gmail.com

or Pothi Sahib open (Parkash) or upside down. You should respectfully close (Santokh) the Gutka Sahib, wrap it up in a Rumala and leave it facing the right way up. By leaving Pothi Sahibs uncovered, they accumulate dust and insects sit upon them.

One should never write any Gurbani on their body, nor even get someone's name written on their body in Gurmukhi. Otherwise, whilst going to the toilet and eating, the Gurmukhi letters are greatly disrespected.

Do not rip pieces of paper out of a notepad or book in which Gurmukhi letters are written, or turn the pages after putting spit on your fingers. Even if you write Gurmukhi letters on a black board, you should not wipe them off with spit. Never sit on any paper with Gurmukhi letters written on it, never touch it with impure (Joothe) hands, never put it on the floor, never put it in your mouth, never roll it up and blow on it with your mouth because your spit goes on it in this way. Never fan yourself with any such papers and do not disrespect them by tapping on them like a tabla drum. Keep your notebooks (with Gurmukhi written in them) in a high place and do not point your feet towards them.

Whichever cupboard, bag or box contains Pothi Sahibs or Gutka Sahibs, do not place glasses, medicines, letters, passports, etc, or anything else in it. Even when in the cupboard, the Pothi Sahibs should not be lower than the bed where you sleep (or any chair you sit on).

You should never place a watch, spectacles, your shoulder or anything else on top of Sri Guru Granth Sahib Jee or a Pothi Sahib. You should not even place a pin on Guru Sahib or a Pothi Sahib. Only Rumalas should be used to stop the Angs from fluttering (due to a gust of wind). All

Kathakaars, writers and virtuous people should uphold this respect.

If we are reading a Pothi Sahib or Gutka Sahib, it does not matter which saintly soul (Mahapurakh) walks in, we should remain seated as upholding the respect for Gurbani, which is being read, is paramount. We should not let anyone bow (Matha Tek) to us and we should not bow to any other human being. The status of Gurbani is esteemed. If anyone tries to bow to you, you should say, "I have Pothi Sahibs with me - bow to them and say the Guru's Fateh loudly to me".

You should not offer any of the following items for bhog (to bless) to Sri Guru Granth Sahib Jee - cannabis, meat, alcohol or tea (due to caffeine).

Some people ridicule those who read Gurbani day and night and say that they do not let Satguru Jee sleep. However, Satguru Jee is always awake. For example:

The True Guru is the awakened Lord
(is always alert/awake).
(Sri Guru Granth Sahib Jee, Ang 479)

For this reason, words that break someone's faith should not be spoken.

At Gurdwara Sri Akhand Parkash in village Bhindran, Brahamgiani Mahapurakhs Sant Baba Sundar Singh Jee Khalsa, Sant Baba Attar Singh Jee and Sant Baba Maghar Singh Jee were discussing which divine Mahapurakh had been blessed with spending time with the most Satgurus. It was discussed that Baba Buddha Sahib Jee was blessed with Darshan of 7 Satgurus and that Baba Budhan Shah was blessed with Darshan of the 1st and 6th

Satguru. Sant Baba Sundar Singh Jee Khalsa folded their hands and said, "This slave firmly believes that anyone who has had Darshan of Sri Guru Granth Sahib Jee, and has meditated upon and understands the Shabad of the Guru, he or she has done complete Darshan of all 10 Paatshaahis." Whenever Sant Baba Sundar Singh Jee used to lift the Rumala from Sri Guru Granth Sahib Jee and do Their Darshan, Baba Jee's face would light up with an extraordinary glow and they would go into ecstasy. Sant Baba Attar Singh Jee said back to them, with hands folded, "We bow to your firm faith."

The souls of Shaheed Singhs stay on guard in the lotus presence of Sri Guru Granth Sahib Jee, to up keep the respect and worship of the Guru of all Gurus, the Saint of all Saints, Satguru Sri Guru Granth Sahib Jee Maharaj. The Shaheed Singhs' souls are quick to help those beloved people who maintain the respect, worship and belief in Guru Sahib Jee.

Only those beloved people, who are blessed by God, uphold the respect for Sri Guru Granth Sahib Jee. Those people who maintain the respect are always graced with peace of mind, which comes with respect for Guru Sahib Jee; we bow humbly again and again to those Gurmukhs.

When holy Saroops of Sri Guru Granth Sahib Jee or Gutka Sahibs and Pothi Sahibs become very old, the Angs rip and Parkash cannot be done; please take them to 'Sri Guru Granth Sahib Bhavan' at Sri Goindwal Sahib where they can be respectfully cremated. This can be done by contacting Damdami Taksal or S.G.P.C (in other countries get in touch with Satkar Committees or local sevadars who may be able to offer help to do this seva).

Khalsa Jeeo! We should respect Satguru Jee's Bani as much as we can, in any way possible; by doing so, Maharaj Jee will bless us with Their unfathomable grace, and Guru Sahib will bestow countless blessings upon us.

Translator's Note

We have attempted to make this publication as close to a word for word translation of the original Gurmukhi version printed by Damdami Taksal (Jatha Bhindran) as possible, with no alterations or additions being made to the text. This English version is not an attempt to replace the original Gurmukhi version, which was authored under the guidance of the Mahapurakhs of Damdami Taksal; rather it is intended to be a stepping-stone for the Sikh youth to turn to for guidance as they begin their path to Sikhi.

We beg for forgiveness from Satguru Sri Guru Granth Sahib Jee Maharaj for any mistakes made whilst translating, publishing, and distributing this publication. May Satguru Jee and the Guru Pyaaree Sadh Sangat kindly forgive our countless errors and continue to bless us with seva of the Khalsa Panth.

Jaskeerth Singh & Sukha Singh (UK)

ANNEXES

Annex 1

Preparing Karah Parshad/Degh

The person who prepares the Karah Parshad should be an Amritdharee who has not committed any of the 4 cardinal sins, does his/her Nitnem, has a daily Ishnaan and keeps the discipline of the five kakkars. The person who is going to make the Degh should have had an ishnaan before preparing the Degh and then thoroughly clean all the utensils to be used, with sand. The kitchen where the Degh is to be prepared should be cleaned and the area of preparation should not have a floor surfaced with cow dung. Cow dung is not to be used in the fire to cook the Degh. All the utensils used are to be of Sarab Loh.

Mool Mantar and Vaheguru Gurmantar are to be continuously recited during the preparation of the Degh. The same volume of sugar, clarified butter, flour (chapatti flour) is all to be added to the Degh (variations of volume are to be made according to how much Degh is needed) and double[82] this amount of water is to be used. The water and sugar are to be brought to the boil in a Karahi (iron wok), once all the sugar has dissolved and the mixture has boiled, this liquid is ready and is to be used later. This mixture can be kept on the stove until needed.

The butter is then added to a Karahi, once it has melted the flour is to be added, then recitation of Sri Japji

---

[82] This is applicable in the West, in India variations may have to be made in the amount of water used, as the sugar is not as refined as it is in the West. More water can be used and the amount needed can be added to the flour that you have roasted in the butter – this may be better to do as sometimes you may heat the water at too high a temperature or leave it on the stove at a high temperature causing more water to evaporate.

Sahib is to commence. The flour and butter are to be roasted, simultaneously Sri Japji Sahib is recited, when the flour has roasted, the mixture previously prepared of water and sugar is to be added. The ingredients are to be mixed thoroughly whilst the liquid mixture is added and the heat reduced to avoid splashes. The Karah Parshad is now prepared and should be put into another utensil if possible, to allow it to cool down. The Karah Parshad should be only taken into the presence of Sri Guru Granth Sahib when it is cool enough to be consumed.

When the Karah Parshad is to be taken into the Darbar Sahib, one Singh is to splash water in front of the Singh carrying the Degh. A rumala is to be placed over the Degh and kept over it at all times. When in the Darbar Sahib, the Degh is to be placed on a table/platform on the right hand side of Sri Guru Granth Sahib Jee. A Singh is then to sit near the Degh and recite the whole Sri Anand Sahib (40 verses); this is for the Bhog of the Degh.

The Bhog to the Degh is to be performed when in the Ardas it is uttered:

I have prepared all sorts of foods in various ways, and all sorts of sweet deserts. I have made my kitchen pure and sacred. Now, O my Lord King, please sample my food. (SGGSJ 1266)

Or when the person doing the Ardas says do Bhog to the Degh, at this point the Kirpan is to be placed into the Degh and withdrawn. The Kirpan is symbolic of the Guru accepting the Degh as weapons are also a form of the Guru. After the Ardas a Hukamnama is read and then the Degh can be distributed to the Sangat. First five handfuls are to be taken out for Panj Pyare (thus the Guru physically eating the Degh), when taking out these initial five

129

handfuls the names of each of the Panj Pyare are to mentally recited, thus Dhan Bhai Deya Singh Jee, Dhan Bhai Dharam Singh Jee, Dhan Bhai Himmat Singh Jee, Dhan Bhai Mokham Singh Jee, Dhan Bhai Sahib Singh Jee. Then one handful of Degh is to be placed in a bowl, covered and placed near to Sri Guru Granth Sahib Jee, this is for the Granthi Singh to consume and is out of respect for the Granthi as he is the minister of the Guru, it is also set aside just in case the Degh runs out. The Degh for the Panj Pyare is to be distributed to 5 Amritdharee Singhs in the sangat, if there aren't 5 Amritdharee Singhs present in the Sangat then the five handfuls are to be mixed back into the Degh. The rest of the Degh is to be equally distributed to the remaining Sangat.

Annex 2

<u>Glossary</u>

Aartee: Can mean two things: A prayer written by Sri Guru Nanak Dev Jee or a type of worship involving ghee lamps, incense and flowers.

Agan Bhet: Cremation.

Akaal Takhat: Highest Seat of Temporal Authority within Sikh Religion. A Gurdwara built by Sri Guru Hargobind Sahib Jee, which is directly opposite to Harmandar Sahib.

Akhand Paath: Continuous recitation of Sri Guru Granth Sahib Jee. Completed within 48 hours.

Amrit: Immortal nectar – which is made from recital of Gurbani (this is the initiation ceremony).

Amritdhari: A person male/female who has become initiated into the Khalsa nation.

Amrit Vela: The hour of Immortal nectar – before sunrise or anytime between 12midnight and 5am.

Ang: Limb, usually used out of respect when referring to Sri Guru Granth Sahib Jee. A Sikh out of respect would say Ang 57 (this is due to Sikhs respecting Sri Guru Granth Sahib as a living Guru).

Anand Sahib: The Prayer of Bliss authored by Sri Guru Amar Das Jee.

Ardaas: Prayer of supplication.

131

Astpadi: A prayer is broken up into Pauree's or Astpadi's, which can be classed as verses, chapters or paragraphs.

Ath-Sath-Ghaat: A place within Sri Darbar Sahib known as the place of 68 pilgrimages.

Bikrami: The original Sikh Calendar.

Bir Asan: Similar to a sprinters stance before a race, the left leg is folded inwardly to rest on and the right leg is to be upright.

Bhai Gurdas Jee: A Brahmgiani Sikh from the time of Sri Guru Arjan Dev Jee. Bhai Sahib was given the duty of being scribe for Guru Jee. Bhai Sahib also wrote Bani of their own which, although is not present in Sri Guru Granth Sahib Jee, should be respected as though it is Gurbani.

Bhatts: A term used for poets who came to the Darbar of Sri Guru Arjan Dev Jee. Their Bani is included in Sri Guru Granth Sahib Jee Maharaj.

Bhog: This word has two meanings. Bhog in relation to food would mean offering the food to Guru Jee. Sri Akhand Paath Bhog would mean the completion of the Sri Akhand Path, so Bhog can mean making a first offering or completion.

Brahmgiani: A saintly person who has the knowledge of God.

Charan: The lotus feet of the Guru.

Chaur Sahib: Whisk waved over Sri Guru Granth Sahib Jee, it is waved over Guru Jee out of respect, in the past such a whisk was waved over the heads of Kings (it is a sign of royalty and respect in the Indian sub-continent and other parts of the world).

Choti Dastar: A small turban worn underneath the main turban. Also referred to as a Keski.

Chola: Sikh gown/warriors dress which is worn by both men and
women.

Daatan: A small twig used to clean teeth.

Damdami Taksal: Institute started by Sri Guru Gobind Singh as a place where the correct pronunciation of Gurbani is taught. Current headquarters are at Gurdwara Gurdarshan Parkash, Amritsar, village Metha.

Darbaar: Court of the Guru, which is the worship hall in a Gurdwara.

Darshan: The blessed vision of the Guru.

Dastar: Turban.

Dharam: Righteousness or Faith.

Dharamraj: Gods ordained servant who is the judge of one's destiny in the next world

Dhoop: Incense.

Dhur Ki Bani: The Divine Word of the Guru coming directly from God.

Gatra: Holster for a Kirpan

Giani: Knowledgeable person or priest.

Granthi: A person who recites the Sri Guru Granth Sahib.

Gupt: Anonymous

Gurbani: Divine word of the Guru (scriptures/prayers).

Gurdwara: Literally meaning "door of the Guru". Refers to the physical place of worship, where Sri Guru Granth Sahib Jee are present.

Gurfateh: Sikh greeting of victory – which is Vaheguru Jee Ka Khalsa, Vaheguru Jee Ki Fateh

Gurmantar: Divine word of the Guru, it is to be meditated upon at all times, this is the word "Vaheguru".

Gurmat: Knowledge of the Guru.

Gurmukhi: This is the Punjabi script that was created by the second Guru, Sri Guru Angad Dev Jee.

Gursikh: Sikh of the Guru.

Gutka: Small anthology of prayers.

Guru(s): Spiritual enlightener – literally Gu means darkness, Ru means light, thus the Guru takes you out of ignorance and enlightens you.

Guru Ka Langar: The kitchen/refectory of the Guru, at which free meals are distributed, without discrimination to all those in attendance.

Harmandar Sahib: Literally meaning the House of God. Commonly referred to as the Golden Temple of Amritsar Sahib.

Hazooree: Presence of the Gurus.

Hukamnama: Command of the Guru.

Ishnaan: Cleansing/bathing and meditating at the same time.

Jaikara: Sound of victory/war cry.

Japji Sahib: First prayer of Sri Guru Granth Sahib, authored by Sri Guru Nanak Dev Jee, recited to gain perfect knowledge of God.

Jathedar: Leader

Jee: Suffix used to signify respect.

Joothe: Impure or unclean.

Jot: A candlelight usually made with Ghee (Clarified Butter).

Joti Jot: Ascension to Sachkhand.

Kacherra: One of the 5K's - knee-length shorts worn for modesty and self-respect.

Kakkar: Articles of faith, namely Kes, Kirpan, Kangha, Kara and Kachera

Kamarkasa: Waste-band

Kaur: Princess – surname of an initiated female Sikh

Karah Parshad: Blessed, sweet, offering, which is distributed at all services/ceremonies in the worship hall of a Gurdwara. It is made of flour, water, sugar and clarified butter, with Japji Sahib being recited during its preparation.

Katha: Religious sermons.

Kathakaar: A person who delivers a religious sermon.

Khalsa: Literally meaning pure - commonly used to refer to Amritdhari Sikhs.

Khalsa Panth: Sikh Nation.

Khanda: Double-edged sword.

Khanda-Batta Amrit: Ambrosial Nectar blessed by the double-edged sword. Given to those who are to be initiated.

Kirpan: Blessed sword – carried by all Amritdhari Sikhs.

Kirtan: Singing Gurbani with the use of instruments, an integral part of Sikh worship.

Kirtan Sohela: Prayer that is recited before a Sikh goes to sleep and recited at the death ceremony of a Sikh.

Manji Sahib: The Throne/seat of the Guru.

Mahapurakh: A saintly person.

Maharaj: Great King.

Maryada: Literally meaning, remembrance of death, Code of Conduct.

Matha Tek: To humbly bow before Sri Guru Granth Sahib Jee.

Mool Mantar: Opening lines of Sri Guru Granth Sahib Jee, literally meaning the essence or root of Sri Guru Granth Sahib Jee, starting with "Ik Oankaar" and ending in "Naanak Hosee Bhee Sach".

Mukhvaakh: The Hukamnama or Command from Sri Guru Granth Sahib Jee

Naam: Divine Name of God, this is Gurbani.

Nirgun: Without physical attributes.

Nitnem: Daily prayers – there are seven in total, consisting of, Japji Sahib, Jaap Sahib, Twai Prasad Swaye (10 verses), Chaupai Sahib, Anand Sahib (40 verses), Rehraas Sahib & Kirtan Sohila. The aforementioned are the minimum prayers to be recited daily; a Sikh can meditate on more prayers as part of their daily recital.

Paath: Recitation of Gurbani.

Paathi: A person who recites Gurbani.

Paatshaah: Great King, (a term used to describe the Guru's) Plural: Paatshaahi.

Palki: Throne.

Panj Ishnaan: Cleansing of hands, face and feet.

Panj Pyare: Five Beloved Ones, they administer the initiation ceremony.

Panj Takhat: Five seats of Authority, namely; Sri Akaal Takhat Sahib, Sri Patna Sahib, Sri Kesgarh Sahib, Sri Damdama Sahib, Sachkhand Sri Hazoor Sahib.

Panna: Page of a religious scripture.

Panth: Nation.

Parchaarak: A person who promotes and educates others on the Sikh Religion.

Parna: Scarf hung loosely around the neck (usually white in colour).

Parkash: Literally meaning, enlighten. Used as a word to describe the ceremony of opening Sri Guru Granth Sahib Jee.

Patase: Sweet puffs that are added to Amrit in the initiation ceremony, they are made with sugar and glucose.

Patka: A small piece of cloth used to cover the head. Normally worn by young children.

Peer: A Muslim saint.

Pehradaar: Guardsman

Pothi(s): Anthology of prayers, vary in sizes but are bigger than Gutkas and smaller than Sri Guru Granth Sahib Jee.

Puratan: Traditional.

Pyaaree: Beloved

Raagmala: Literally meaning "The Rosary of Love." The concluding prayer of Sri Guru Granth Sahib Jee.

Ragi: Person that performs Kirtan.

Rehat: Discipline/Way of life.

Rehat Maryada: Literally meaning, the remembering of death. Code of conduct.

Rehatnama: Code of conduct.

Rehraas Sahib: Evening prayer.

Rumala: Clothing of Sri Guru Granth Sahib Jee.

S.G.P.C: Shiromani Gurdwara Parbandhak Committee.

Sachkhand: The state of Truth.

Sadh Sangat: Congregation of Saints/Sikhs, where only the name of God is meditated or discussed.

Sahib: Literally meaning, Master – often used as a suffix.

Sahibzada: Son of the Guru.

Samparda: Sikh Institution.

Sangat: Congregation.

Sangrand: First day of a new month according to the solar calendar.

Sant: A Sikh saint.

Santokh: Literally meaning contentment. A term used when Sri Guru Granth Sahib Jee is resting.

Sarab Loh: Pure iron

Sargun: With attributes.

Saroop: An edition of Sri Guru Granth Sahib Jee

Sarovar: Sacred pool, sarovars usually adjoin Gurdwaras where Sikhs/pilgrims bathe.

Satguru: True Guru – the Sikh Gurus.

Sehaj Paath: The complete recital of Sri Guru Granth Sahib Jee, which is completed in intervals (no time restriction for completion is imposed).

Seva: Selfless service performed to attain the merit of God's grace or the blessing of other Sikhs; no worldly reward is attached to doing Seva.

Sevadaar: A person who carries out selfless service.

Shabad: Prayers written by the Gurus.

Shaheed: Sikh Martyr.

Shastar: Weapons.

Shudh: Complete or correct.

Shudh Santhia: Complete or proficient pronunciation of Gurbani.

Sidhs: A group of saints/wise men who practised yoga and lived in mountains.

Sikhi: Practice of the Sikh faith.

Simran: Meditation.

Singh: Lion – surname of an initiated Sikh male.

Sri: Prefix meaning, supreme (short for shiromani).

Sri Dasam Granth Sahib Jee: Anthology of Sikh hymns written by Sri Guru Gobind Singh Jee.

Sri Guru Granth Sahib Jee: The Guru of the Sikhs, anthology of Sikh hymns.

Sukhaasan/Sukhasan: Literally meaning the posture of bliss. A term used when Sri Guru Granth Sahib Jee is resting.

Tabiya/Taabiyaa: Guru Jee's Platform.

Tankhaah: Punishment – administered by the Panj Pyare.

Teeya: A day when Indian women would get together in the village and dance. This is completely against Sikh beliefs.

Vaheguru: Literally meaning the Wonderous Lord. One of many terms used to describe God. (This is the Gurmantar).

Vidiya: Education

Abbreviations

SGGSJ – Sri Guru Granth Sahib Jee

<u>The Sikh Guru's</u>

Sri Guru Nanak Dev Jee
Sri Guru Angad Dev Jee
Sri Guru Amar Das Jee
Sri Guru Ram Das Jee
Sri Guru Arjan Dev Jee
Sri Guru Hargobind Sahib Jee
Sri Guru Har Rai Sahib Jee
Sri Guru Har Krishan Sahib Jee
Sri Guru Tegh Bahadur Sahib Jee
Sri Guru Gobind Singh Jee
Sri Guru Granth Sahib Jee